EUROPEAN POLITICAL, ECONOMIC, AND SECURITY ISSUES

ROMANIA

ENVIRONMENTAL, SOCIAL AND ECONOMIC ISSUES

European Political, Economic, and Security Issues

Additional books and e-books in this series can be found on Nova's website under the Series tab.

European Political, Economic, and Security Issues

Romania

Environmental, Social and Economic Issues

Sophie Clarke
Editor

Copyright © 2018 by Nova Science Publishers, Inc.
All rights reserved. No part of this book may be reproduced, stored in a retrieval system or transmitted in any form or by any means: electronic, electrostatic, magnetic, tape, mechanical photocopying, recording or otherwise without the written permission of the Publisher.

We have partnered with Copyright Clearance Center to make it easy for you to obtain permissions to reuse content from this publication. Simply navigate to this publication's page on Nova's website and locate the "Get Permission" button below the title description. This button is linked directly to the title's permission page on copyright.com. Alternatively, you can visit copyright.com and search by title, ISBN, or ISSN.

For further questions about using the service on copyright.com, please contact:
Copyright Clearance Center
Phone: +1-(978) 750-8400 Fax: +1-(978) 750-4470 E-mail: info@copyright.com.

NOTICE TO THE READER

The Publisher has taken reasonable care in the preparation of this book, but makes no expressed or implied warranty of any kind and assumes no responsibility for any errors or omissions. No liability is assumed for incidental or consequential damages in connection with or arising out of information contained in this book. The Publisher shall not be liable for any special, consequential, or exemplary damages resulting, in whole or in part, from the readers' use of, or reliance upon, this material. Any parts of this book based on government reports are so indicated and copyright is claimed for those parts to the extent applicable to compilations of such works.

Independent verification should be sought for any data, advice or recommendations contained in this book. In addition, no responsibility is assumed by the publisher for any injury and/or damage to persons or property arising from any methods, products, instructions, ideas or otherwise contained in this publication.

This publication is designed to provide accurate and authoritative information with regard to the subject matter covered herein. It is sold with the clear understanding that the Publisher is not engaged in rendering legal or any other professional services. If legal or any other expert assistance is required, the services of a competent person should be sought. FROM A DECLARATION OF PARTICIPANTS JOINTLY ADOPTED BY A COMMITTEE OF THE AMERICAN BAR ASSOCIATION AND A COMMITTEE OF PUBLISHERS.

Additional color graphics may be available in the e-book version of this book.

Library of Congress Cataloging-in-Publication Data
Names: Clarke, Sophie editor.
Title: Romania : environmental, social and economic issues / editor, Sophie Clarke.
Description: Hauppauge, New York : Nova Science Publisher's, Inc., 2017. |
Series: European political, economic, and security issues | Includes bibliographical references and index.
Identifiers: LCCN 2018047550 (print) | LCCN 2018048611 (ebook) | ISBN 9781536145915 (ebook) | ISBN 9781536145908 (softcover)
Subjects: LCSH: Romania--Politics and government--20th century. | Goga, Octavian, 1881-1938. | Romania--Environmental conditions. | Geotourism--Romania--Banat Mountains. | Renewable energy sources--Romania.
Classification: LCC DR266 (ebook) | LCC DR266 .R59 2017 (print) | DDC 333.709498--dc23
LC record available at https://lccn.loc.gov/2018047550

Published by Nova Science Publishers, Inc. † New York

CONTENTS

PREFACE

Geodiversity is a topic widely researched around the globe and numerous studies have been developed in recent years based on geodiversity and related topics such as geomorphosites and geotourism. In Romania: Environmental, Social and Economic Issues, the authors highlight the diversity of geosites in Anina Mountains, Romania and the role of this high geodiversity in environmental protection, education and socio-economic development. Next, the authors discuss the interest in "green" technology from the authorities and inhabitants of Romania. Additionally, in Romania there is an increasing interest in building with low pollution, high efficiency and environmental friendliness. In closing, the authors discuss the political crisis of December, 1937 in Romania which caused the formation of the government of O. Goga, the chairman of the National Christian Party. The activities of the government were also interrupted by the King's decision to establish authoritativeness on February 11, 1938.

Chapter 1 - Geodiversity is a topic widely researched around the globe and numerous studies have been developed in the last years based on geodiversity and related topics such as geomorphosites and geotourism. Moreover, geodiversity is addressed from various perspectives, such as environmental protection, tourism development and its role in public education and awareness. There are different approaches regarding geomorphosites assessments, but all these approaches agree that geosites may have a significant role in nature protection, public awareness, and education. Anina Mountains are located in the most compact and largest surface of carbonate rocks in Romania, namely Reşiţa-Moldova Nouă Synclinorium. Besides, Anina Mountains benefit from a rich diversity in geomorphologic sites, especially in karst landforms; those may be considered as geomorphosites. A large diversity of karst landforms such as springs, caves, gorges and karst plateaus with a high density of karst features, are found within the study area. The presence of these geosites may improve natural features protection and economic development of this region. The aim of this study is to highlight the high diversity of geosites in Anina Mountains, Romania and the roles of this high geodiversity in environmental protection, education and socio-economic development of this region. After a thorough research in the field and a detailed literature review, the present study's conclusions bring into public awareness the positive role of geodiversity in nature conservation, education and socio-economic development in Anina Mountains.

Chapter 2 - In this chapter author's evidence main aspects of the interest in "green" (energy, motion/mobility, building/construction) – from the authorities and, maybe most important, from the inhabitants of Romania, at the end of second decade of XXI centrury. First, there should be mentioned the interest in producing green energy, especially renewable one, solar energy. There are a lot of funds allocated to scientifc research and, consequently, to its applied results with benefits and commercial potential. Thus, an innovative equipment designed and prototyped so as to obtain solar cells (based on perovskite) with PCE (Power conversion efficiency) not less than 15%, is presented. Another aspect of Romania's green trend is that of electric e-motion. It is about the population interest in buying and, further, using electric bikes, hybrid or, completely, electric cars and, consequently, SMEs involvement in installing e-charging stations – all over countryside. For the moment, the focus is on public parking (in hypermarkets, malls) and on main fuel stations of the main providers (OMV, Rompetrol, Petrom, etc.). Last, but not least, in Romania there is an increasing interest in building with low pollution, high efficiency and environmental friendly. LGS (Light Gauge Steel) load bearing systems are the ones used in building houses, industrial halls, silos and farms, so that they are ecological and sustainable. Some aspects of scientific research, as well as its application and benefits in manufacturing LGS profiles, when building “metallic” houses, are evidenced. Bottom line, nowadays Romania is looking towards green – in the terms of environmental friendly, efficiency, user friendly and, why not, less expensive, even on long term.

Chapter 3 - The political crisis of December 1937 in Romania caused the formation of the government of O. Goga, the chairman of the National Christian Party. The personal decision of the King Carol II gave hope for a long reign, in connection with which intensive preparations for the new parliamentary elections were held. The activities of the government were also interrupted by the King's decision to establish authoritatively on February 11 1938.

In: Romania
Editor: Sophie Clarke
ISBN: 978-1-53614-590-8
© 2018 Nova Science Publishers, Inc.

Chapter 1

THE ROLE OF GEODIVERSITY IN ENVIRONMENTAL PROTECTION, ECONOMIC DEVELOPMENT AND EDUCATION IN THE ANINA MOUNTAINS, ROMANIA

Laurenţiu Artugyan*
Independent Researcher, Romania

ABSTRACT

Geodiversity is a topic widely researched around the globe and numerous studies have been developed in the last years based on geodiversity and related topics such as geomorphosites and geotourism. Moreover, geodiversity is addressed from various perspectives, such as environmental protection, tourism development and its role in public education and awareness. There are different approaches regarding geomorphosites assessments, but all these approaches agree that geosites may have a significant role in nature protection, public awareness, and education. Anina Mountains are located in the most compact and largest

* Corresponding Author: Laurenţiu Artugyan, PhD in Geography, non-affiliated, Freelance Science Writer; Email: lau_artugyan@yahoo.com.

surface of carbonate rocks in Romania, namely Reşiţa-Moldova Nouă Synclinorium. Besides, Anina Mountains benefit from a rich diversity in geomorphologic sites, especially in karst landforms; those may be considered as geomorphosites. A large diversity of karst landforms such as springs, caves, gorges and karst plateaus with a high density of karst features, are found within the study area. The presence of these geosites may improve natural features protection and economic development of this region. The aim of this study is to highlight the high diversity of geosites in Anina Mountains, Romania and the roles of this high geodiversity in environmental protection, education and socio-economic development of this region. After a thorough research in the field and a detailed literature review, the present study's conclusions bring into public awareness the positive role of geodiversity in nature conservation, education and socio-economic development in Anina Mountains.

Keywords: geodiversity, geosites, economic development, education, Anina Mountains, Romania

INTRODUCTION

The large variety of Earth's surface materials, landforms and physical processes having scientific value is known as geodiversity. Besides its scientific value, geodiversity has other important benefits for human society, especially in Earth evolution understanding or climate change (Gray, 2013). These values of geodiversity started to be linked with landscape conservation, sustainable development, economic progress and people's wellbeing (Hjort et al., 2015). According to Panizza (2009), the term "geodiversity" should be used for those landscapes those are unique and different from other landscapes from the geological perspective.

Features those are part of geodiversity include the geological structure, soil, relief, surface water, underground cavities, underground water and the impact of these features towards biotic elements and climate. These components can be summarized in one word – landscape. Consequently, geodiversity is focused to preserve the natural landscape (Alexandrowicz and Kozlowski, 1999).

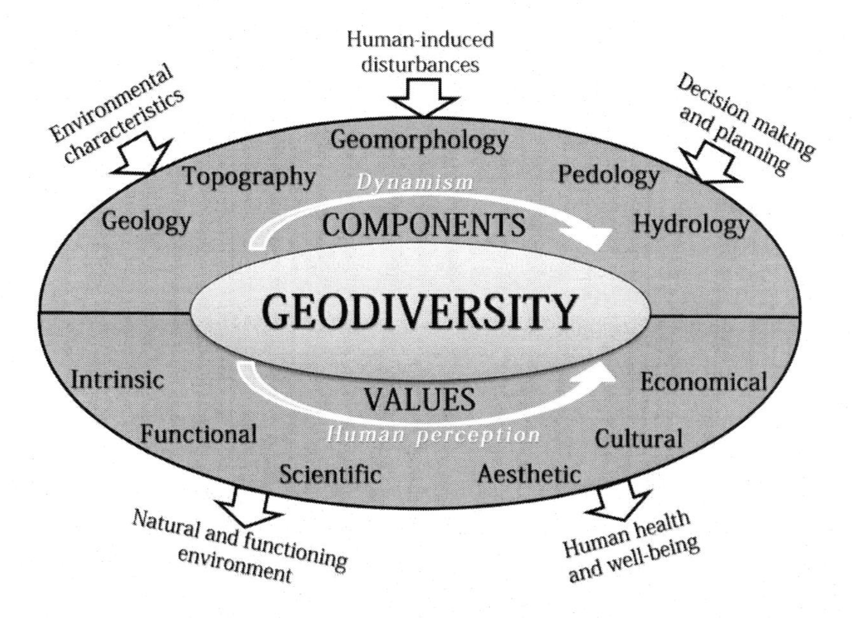

Figure 1. The main components and values of geodiversity and their key influences (modified after Gray 2013; Gray et al., 2013).

The major components of geodiversity include geology, topography, geomorphology, pedology, and hydrology. All these components together are very dynamic and create different landscapes. Landscapes created by the above-mentioned components of geodiversity generate in human perception different values, such as intrinsic, functional, scientific, aesthetic, cultural and economic values (Figure 1).

The concept of geodiversity points out both sensitivity of abiotic elements and the dynamic and vulnerability of geological, geomorphological and nature protection in land development and management (Erhartič and Zorn, 2012). Geodiversity is focused on protecting the lithosphere of the Earth, counteracting, preventing and eliminating those factors caused by human activities that can threaten geodiversity (Alexandrowicz and Kozlowski, 1999).

Gray et al., (2013) mention that geodiversity and geoscience bring an essential contribution to deliver integrated ecosystem management by providing solutions to a wide range of issues in domains like environmental, economic and social life.

Geodiversity is a topic widely researched around the globe and numerous studies have been developed in the last years (Dowling, 2011) based on geodiversity and related topics such as geomorphosites and geotourism (Serrano and González-Trueba, 2005; Panizza, 2009; Erhartič, 2010; Pereira and Pereira, 2010; Feuillet and Sourp, 2011; Coratza et al., 2012; Zgłobicki and Baran-Zgłobicka, 2013; Miccadei et al., 2014; Kubalíková and Kirchner, 2015).

Moreover, geodiversity is addressed from various perspectives, such as environmental protection and sustainable development (Hose, 2007; Ghiraldi et al., 2009; Erhartič and Zorn, 2012; Raharimahefa, 2012; Dowling, 2013; Comer et al., 2015; Forleo et al., 2017; Chakrabarty and Mandal, 2018), economic and tourism development (Farsani et al., 2010; Farsani et al., 2011; Gordon and Barron, 2012; Zhyrnov, 2015; Abdel Maksoud and Hussien, 2016; Safarabadi and Shahzeidi, 2018) and its role in public education and awareness (Zouros, 2010; Bollati et al., 2011; Pelfini and Bollati, 2014; Lukic et al., 2016).

There are different approaches regarding geomorphosites assessments (Brilha, 2016), but all these approaches agree that geosites may have a significant role in nature protection, public awareness, and education.

In the recent years, geomorphosites started to be more discussed in Romania. Moreover, geodiversity and role of geosites in tourism development have become an important topic among Romanian researchers.

We may mention here some of the studies those are focused on geomorphosites and geosites evaluation in different Romanian regions, such as Comănescu and Dobre (2009), Comănescu and Nedelea (2010), Gavrilă et al., (2011), Ilinca and Comănescu (2011), Comănescu et al., (2012, 2013), Gavrilă and Anghel (2013), and Comănescu et al., (2017). Studies focused on karst geomorphosites are less numerous and we may mention Crişan et al., (2015), Artugyan (2017), Iamandei (2017) and Cocean and Cocean (2017).

On the other hand, roles of geodiversity and geomorphosites in education, tourism development, economic progress and environmental protection in Romania are sporadically discussed in few studies, such as

Comănescu and Dobre (2009), Purice et al., (2013), Necheş (2013), Artugyan (2014), and Necheş and Erdeli (2015).

The aim of this study is to highlight the high diversity of geosites in Anina Mountains, Romania and the roles of this high geodiversity in environmental protection, education and socio-economic development of this region.

Even if geotourism and geomorphosites have become a topic more attractive in Romania in recent years among scientists, most of the studies are focused on well-known touristic areas, such as Bucegi Mountains, Măcin Mountains or Bucureşti City.

However, Anina Mountains have a wide range of geosites those may be considered extremely attractive among tourists. These geosites are part of karst landscapes that are specific for this region. Consequently, this study proposes an incursion into a less known region benefiting from a rich geodiversity.

Geotourists are interested to examine and admire breathtaking, unique and remarkable landscapes and geological sites, especially in the field, but also inside the museums. Furthermore, geotourism can promote geosites conservation. Moreover, geotourism can fund the development of local communities and conservation of the geosites (Hose, 2007).

Since karst environment is among the most vulnerable landscape on the Earth, it is highly recommended that the entire range of human activities developed within this landscape promotes sustainability and ecology.

If in the past the most threatening human activities towards karst environment were deforestation, mining, agriculture and water exploitation, nowadays tourism and recreational activities are among other human activities those may threat karst landscape (Hoyos et al., 1998).

BRIEF DESCRIPTION OF THE STUDY AREA

The study area of this research, namely Anina Mountains, is situated in the south-western part of Romania, in Caraş-Severin County, being a subunit of Banat Mountains, having a northwest-southeast orientation (Figure 2).

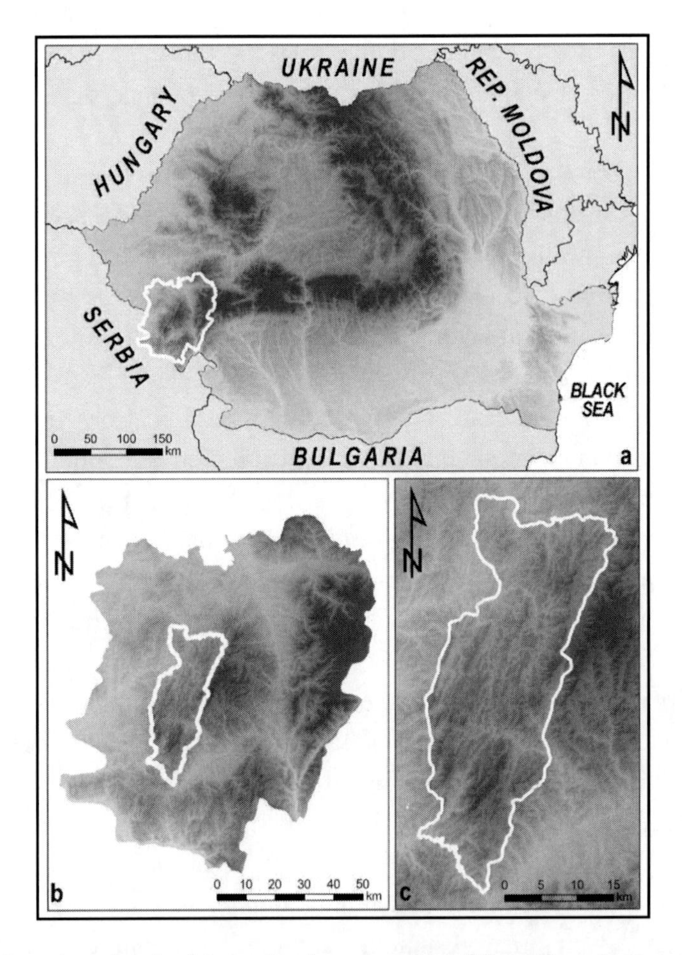

Figure 2. Location of Anina Mountains Area: location of Caraş-Severin County (a); location of Anina Mountains in Caraş-Severin County (b) and detailed view of Anina Mountains (c).

Limits of Anina Mountains are following mostly natural features. In the northern part, the limit is represented by Bârzava River. The eastern limit is formed also by a sector of Bârzava River, which separates Anina Mountains and Semenic Mountains, Poneasca Valley and the border between carbonate rocks of Anina Mountains and non-carbonate rocks of Bozovici Hills. In the southern part, the limit is represented by Nera

Valley, while the western limit is represented by the contact between limestone of Anina Mountains and Oraviţa Hills, the valleys of Lupac and Bârzaviţa creeks (Sencu, 1978).

Anina Mountains are located in the most compact and largest surface of carbonate rocks in Romania, namely Reşiţa-Moldova Nouă Synclinorium (Orăşeanu and Iurkiewicz, 2010). Almost 2% of Romania surface is covered by limestone (Sencu, 1978), this percent representing almost 4,500 square kilometers (Orghidan, 1972).

Different types of limestone are found in Anina Mountains at different stratigraphic levels, forming large surfaces of limestone. These mountains are part of a folded region, with numerous anticlines and synclines, having a Jurassian relief (Mateescu, 1961).

The geomorphological characteristics are imposed by the geological structure of this region. Long parallel ridges are separated by deep valleys and karst plateaus (Bucur, 1997). These karst plateaus are representative of suspended karst plateaus characterized by wide and flat interfluves separated by deep valleys. Moreover, these suspended karst plateaus are characterized by a high degree of karstification (Onac, 2000).

Besides, Anina Mountains benefit from a rich diversity in geomorphologic sites, mostly karst landforms, as a consequence of high diversity of lithology (Răileanu et al., 1964). Numerous of these geomorphologic sites may be considered as geomorphosites. A large diversity of karst landforms such as springs, caves, gorges and karst plateaus with a high density of karst features, are found within the study area (Artugyan, 2017). Tufa and travertine can be found also in this region, being other two elements of geodiversity (Hjort et al., 2015). Moreover, fossiliferous areas and wonderful lakes add even more attractiveness and interest to this region.

As a consequence of the richness and diversity of landforms and biodiversity, two national parks were developed in Anina Mountains, namely Semenic – Caraş Gorges National Park and Nera Gorges – Beuşniţa National Park. These two national parks share one common border, the southern border for Semenic – Caraş Gorges National Park being common with the northern border of Nera Gorges – Beuşniţa National Park.

The fact that those two protected areas share one common border has a highly positive impact on environmental protection and geotourism development since a large area is governed by strict laws regarding the environmental protection. Moreover, these two national parks give compactness and continuity for protected areas having similar characteristics like landscape, biodiversity, cultural aspects and geology.

The presence of these two national parks within the Anina Mountains represents a favorable factor for the development of geotourism, environmental education and tourism development based on ecologic assumptions.

As for the most important communities part of the Anina Mountains, we have to mention smalls town like Anina and Oraviţa, and numerous rural communities. Among the largest rural communities, we may mention Bozovici, Caraşova, Sasca Montană, Şopotu Nou, Ciclova Română, Ciclova Montană, Cărbunari, and Ciudanoviţa. All these communities represent the gates through different geosites located within Anina Mountains.

History of Anina Mountains region is strongly related to forestry and coal mining. Most of the above-mentioned communities have been settled after important coal resources were discovered in this region. After communism failed in Romania in 1989, the mining sector has declined in the entire country and Anina Mountains region was not an exception. All these communities suffered from poverty, depopulation, and lack of identity after mining activity has totally stopped around the year of 2000.

Statistics highlight very well the important percent of people who left these communities in Anina Mountains (Figure 3). Moreover, numerous people who have left are not included in these statistics, since they still have their residence in these communities, but in fact, they are working and living abroad for several years. The most affected are the children who are still in these communities, living without their parents. The school population has decreased considerably also in the communities in Anina

Mountains, showing that the future of these communities is quite dismal (Figure 4).

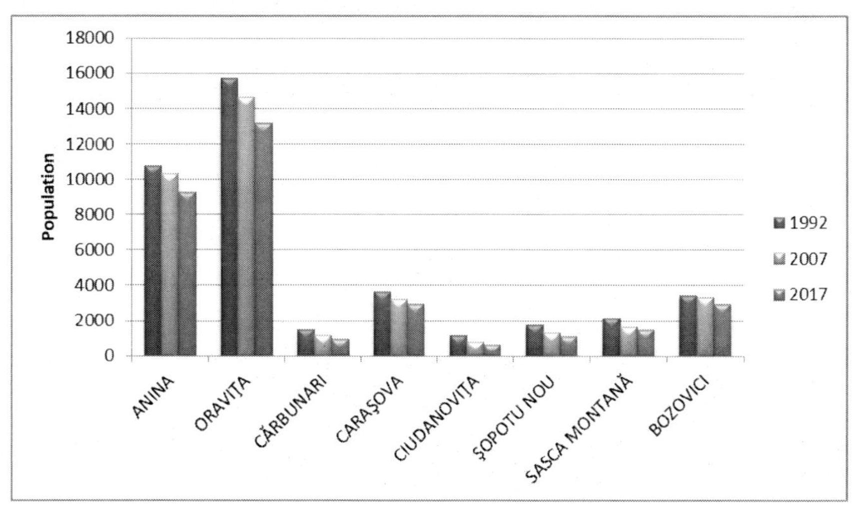

Data source: National Institute of Statistics.

Figure 3. Population evolution in the major communities within Anina Mountains between 1992 and 2017.

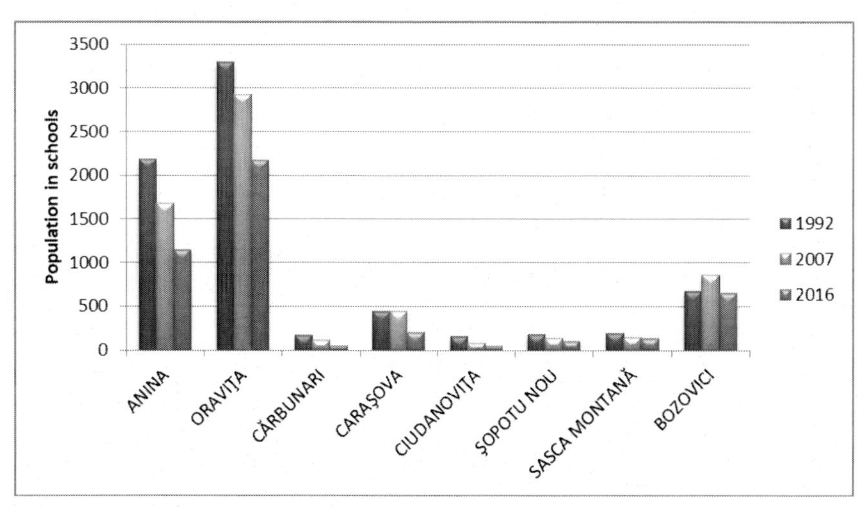

Data source: National Institute of Statistics.

Figure 4. Population in schools evolution in the major communities within Anina Mountains between 1992 and 2016.

Despite the fact that numerous people have left these communities, tourism started to become an important domain for the revitalization of this region. This aspect is proved by the numerous accommodation spaces developed in the last years. If the socialist regime left numerous accommodation spaces, these lodging spaces were abandoned and after 10 years of capitalism tourism in this region was almost a closed subject. However, after the year of 2010 numerous pensions have been developed. For example, in Anina town, during the first visit in this town in 2007, only 1 pension was functioning and two other hotels were abandoned. Today, in 2018, during the last visit in the field, in March 2018, 8 pensions were counted and other 2 are about to be opened soon. This is a good proof that tourism is developing in this region.

Another proof that tourism started to become more important for this region is represented by the number of tourists mentioned in the statistics (Figure 5). Unfortunately, very often these tourists are not reported by pensions' administrators and consequently, the numbers present in the statistics are not complete.

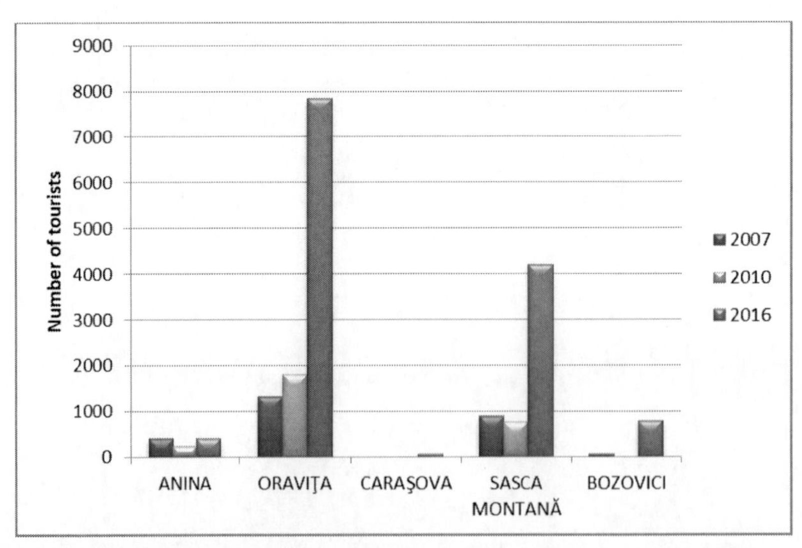

(Data source: National Institute of Statistics).

Figure 5. Number of tourists in the major communities within Anina Mountains between 2007 and 2016.

Geotourism Sites in Anina Mountains

Anina Mountains have numerous geosites and geotourism may represent a great chance for the revitalization of this region in Romania. The most representative and best knew features belonging to the geomorphological heritage as geosites in these mountains have been chosen, being represented as points and areal (Table 1). These geosites are spatially represented on the map in Figure 6.

Table 1. Major geosites in Anina Mountains, listed from north to south

No.	Name	Type
1	Caraş Gorges	Areal
2	Bats Cave	Point
3	Comarnic Cave	Point
4	Mărghitaş Karstic Plateau	Areal
5	Gârlişte Gorges	Areal
6	The Cave with Water from Gârlişte Gorges	Point
7	Buhui Cave	Point
8	Caraş Spring	Point
9	Zânei Hill (Tâlva Zânei)	Areal
10	Ponor Cave	Point
11	Plopa Cave	Point
12	Miniş Gorges	Areal
13	Bigăr Spring and Bigăr Waterfall	Point
14	Beuşniţa Valley	Areal
15	Beuşniţa Waterfalls	Point
16	Ochiul Bei Lake	Point
17	Văioaga Waterfall	Point
18	Moceriş Waterfall	Point
19	Devil's Lake	Point
20	Nera Gorges	Areal

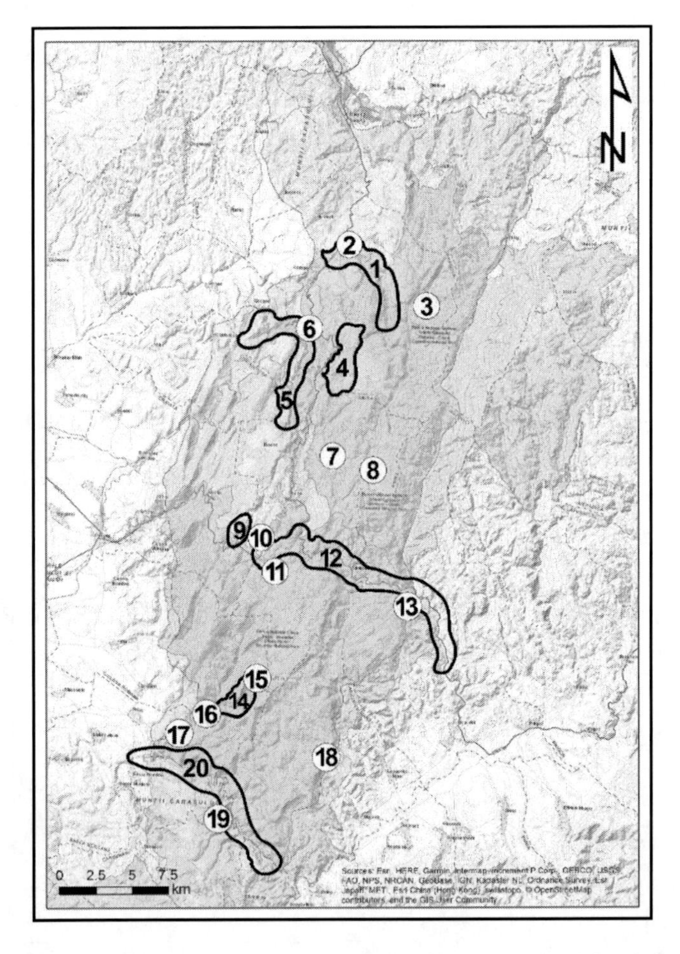

Figure 6. Location of the most important geosites within the Anina Mountains: 1-Caraş Gorges; 2-Bats Cave; 3-Comarnic Cave; 4-Mărghitaş Karstic Plateau; 5-Gârlişte Gorges; 6-The Cave with Water from Gârlişte Gorges; 7-Buhui Cave; 8-Caraş Spring; 9-Zânei Hill (Tâlva Zânei); 10-Ponor Cave; 11-Plopa Cave; 12-Miniş Gorges; 13-Bigăr Spring and Bigăr Waterfall; 14-Beuşniţa Valley; 15-Beuşniţa Waterfalls; 16-Ochiu Bei Lake; 17-Văioaga Waterfall; 18-Moceriş Waterfall; 19-Devil's Lake; 20-Nera Gorges.

These geosites contain numerous superlatives of Romanian karst landscapes. Nera Gorges represent the longest sector of gorges in Romania, having 22 km long between Sasca Montană and Şopotu Nou. Moreover, Devil's Lake, which is situated at the middle distance of Nera Gorges, is the biggest natural karstic lake in Romania. Another karst lake, which is unique in this part of the country, is Ochiu Bei Lake. This lake is powered by water from an underground spring and consequently, this lake never freezes.

Going further, waterfalls formed on calcareous tufa are very numerous and spectacular. Beuşniţa, Văioaga, Moceriş, and Bigăr waterfalls are among the most attractive tourist sites in the south-western part of Romania and maybe in the entire country. It should be highlighted that recently Bigăr Waterfall has been considered to be among the most beautiful waterfalls in the world. The consequence is that the numbers of visitors all over the world have grown very quickly and during the weekends this place is overcrowded.

Besides the calcareous tufa, another feature specific to this area is represented by travertine. Small travertine dams can be found along Buhui Creek in Buhui Gorges, at the Caraş Spring and the most spectacular travertine dams are seen along Beuşniţa Valley, forming numerous rapids of travertine and wonderful small waterfalls.

Karst springs are also representative for this region, mentioning here Caraş Spring, which is the "birth" place of the river that forms spectacular Caraş Gorges several kilometers downstream, or Bigăr Spring. In order to reach Bigăr Spring and Bigăr Waterfalls, you must pass through fantastic gorges sectors, namely Miniş Gorges. The largest part of Miniş Gorges is crossed by the national road DN57B, which facilitates the access to this part of Anina Mountains.

Zânei Hill (or Tâlva Zânei how it is called in the local dialect) is another great geosite in the area. Part of this hill was used as a quarry in the past, but nowadays it is abandoned. This hill contains numerous Jurassic plant fossils (Popa and Meller 2009) and based on these fossils, this site was proposed as geopark in order to increase the preservation of these Jurassic fossils (Popa et al., 2010).

Mărghitaş Karstic Plateau is a representative suspended karstic plateau (Onac, 2000), being separated by the other karst plateaus by the deep valley formed by Buhui Creek. Mărghitaş Karstic Plateau includes numerous specific karst features, such as sinkholes, sinkhole valleys, dry valleys, blind valleys, and potholes.

Besides these geosites those are at the surface of the Earth, Anina Mountains “hosts” also numerous breathtaking and unique caves. The most important caves are Comarnic, Buhui, Plopa, Ponor Bats' Cave and the Cave with Water from Gârlişte Gorges. Comarnic Cave is the largest cave in the Banat Mountains, being the only one cave having the minimum tourist facilities. Buhui Cave is the 2nd largest cave in Banat Mountains, being crossed by the homonymous creek, which is one of the longest underground rivers in Romania. Ponor Cave and Plopa Cave are situated in Miniş Gorges. Ponor and Plopa caves are part of large underground karst system, these two caves being crossed by Ponor Creek. Ponor Cave is the dry, fossil level of Ponor-Plopa Karst System, while Plopa Cave is the active level of this underground karst system (Sencu, 1964). Ponor Cave attracts due to numerous big speleothems and some cave pearls, while Plopa Cave is spectacular due to several very large rimstone dams and rimstone pools formed near the entrance of the cave. Moreover, Plopa Cave, also known as Bones Cave or Peştera cu Oase (in Romanian) represents also an extremely important paleontological site, since in this cave were found in 2002 some of the oldest humans remains in Europe (Trinkaus et al., 2003a; Trinkaus et al., 2003b). Bats' Cave is one of the biggest caves in Caraş Gorges, being quite accessible for tourists, while Cave with Water from Gârlişte Gorges is another spectacular cave in Anina Mountains. Cave with Water from Gârlişte Gorges attracts due to numerous rimstone dams and bats colonies living there. Besides, the water flowing through the cave is coming from several sinkholes situated on one suspended karstic plateau situated above the cave. Gârlişte Gorges represent one of the most spectacular and wild sectors of gorges in the entire country, having 9 km long.

Besides the geomorphological and geological attraction, some of the above-described geosites attract due to wonderful legends. Because some of these geomorphosites are linked to the history of these places through legends and legendary local characters, the cultural value of these geosites is higher due to these legends. Consequently, these geomorphosites may attract more tourists, since not all kind of tourists are interested only in geological and geomorphological aspects. Among tourists may be numerous people interested to discover the local history and local legends.

Figure 7 and Figure 8 present photos' collages including most of the above-mentioned geosites within Anina Mountains.

During the peak season, the tourist trails leading to these sites are full of tourists of all ages. Most of these geosites can be reached using numerous marked tourist paths, but some of them are not placed along the marked trails.

Figure 7. Pictures of main geomorphosites in the northern part of Anina Mountains: 1-Gârlişte Gorges; 2-Bigăr Waterfall; 3-Caraş Spring; 4-Bigăr Spring; 5-Caraş Gorges; 6-Jurrasic flora fossil in Zânei Hill; 7-Buhui Cave entrance; 8-Caraş Gorges seen from above; 9-The Cave with Water in Gârlişte Gorges; 10-Scenic view above Mărghitaş Karstic Plateau; 11-Sinkhole valley and dry valley in Mărghitaş Karstic Plateau.

Figure 8. Pictures of main geomorphosites in the southern part of Anina Mountains: 1-Ochiu Bei Lake; 2-Nera Gorges; 3-Plopa Cave; 4-Văioaga Waterfall; 5-Miniş Gorges; 6-Beuşniţa Valley; 7-Beuşniţa Waterfall during the dry season; 8- Beuşniţa Waterfall during the rainy season; 9-Beuşniţa Valley at the confluence with Beu Valley; 10-Bats Cave; 11-Devil's Lake.

Besides the above mentioned geosites, Anina Mountains attract numerous tourists due to other great attractions, such as Buhui Lake, which is the first lake built on karst terrain in Romania in 1904, Mărghitaş Lake, which is the first lake built for leisure in Romania in 1911, Anina – Oraviţa Railway, which is the first mountainous railway built in Romania after the model of Austrian Semmering. This railway is built in the mountains, having 14 tunnels and 10 viaducts, the railway having 33 km long.

Moreover, Anina Mountains have more than 600 caves (Goran, 1982), which represent one of the highest densities of caves in Romania.

According to Pralong (2005), geomorphosites are evaluated from the tourist perspective based on the following criteria: aesthetic, scientific, cultural or historical and economic. Aesthetic and scientific criteria are intrinsic values given by the representativeness, uniqueness, and importance of each geosite. The cultural or historic criterion is given by the events, religious importance or archeological relevance, while the economic criterion is related to the accessibility to each geosite, natural risks, the annual number of visitors, the attraction generated by each geosite and the level of protection of each geosite.

If the geomorphosites in Anina Mountains are considered as very attractive and in most of the cases the level protection for each site is very high, unfortunately, the accessibility aspect is an important minus for these sites. Even most of the geosites can be reached by roads and paths, very numerous roads are almost impracticable, especially in the area of Sasca Montană, Potoc, and Cărbunari. The accessibility part should be considerably improved in order to bring an important economic development for this region since most of the owners of accommodation claim that numerous tourists don't come back to these regions due to the bad roads.

METHODOLOGY

The main goal of this research is to identify the roles of geodiversity in environmental protection, education and economic development in Anina Mountains. In order to reach the goal of this paper, a methodology combining relevant literature and numerous field applications is proposed.

The methodology of this research has three distinct phases: the first phase consists of an extensive literature review regarding geosites, karst geomorphosites and the role of geotourism in different parts of the world; the second phase represents numerous field trips in the studied area to observe and photograph the most important geosites, while the third phase is focused on strategies and suggestions regarding the role of geomorphosites and geotourism in local economic growth, educational and cultural progress, and environmental protection.

After several field applications, the most representative geosites those may be seen in Anina Mountains were considered as a great opportunity for the development of this region. Besides, since a large surface of this mountainous area is part of two national parks, environmental protection may be enhanced at the same time with the tourism promotion and economic development. Consequently, during several years we have visited the most attractive and best-known geomorphological sites trying to find the best solutions to come up with reliable suggestions and strategies.

Moreover, during the field work, discussions with local people gave us the perspective of local inhabitants regarding the presence of significant geologic features, unique landscapes and attractive geosites in their region. In order to support our strategies on reliable studies, a rich bibliography was read and the most valuable findings that may be adapted to the reality of the studied area were proposed for the geodiversity of Anina Mountains.

ROLES OF GEOPARKS

Quoting Mc Keever and Zouros (2005), geoparks are defined as "places where the amazing story of our planet can be told to the non-specialist without the need for the use of the esoteric language so often employed by geoscientists" (Mc Keever and Zouros, 2005, p. 274).

Geoparks can support the socio-cultural development of local communities by holding festivals, workshops, fairs, different educational programs and introducing local cultural traditions to visitors. Consequently, geotourism can promote more than geological heritage, promoting local food, handicrafts businesses, and cultural preservation. All these aspects may include geoparks as a pillar in the development of sustainable tourism (Farsani et al., 2011).

Geoparks are great places to develop formal education activities for the general public, having an important role in the Earth Sciences education.

By involving geoparks in the educational process, geodiversity and the geological value of a site may be easier understood. Moreover, through geoparks, it is highly promoted geoconservation (Henriques et al., 2012). Geoconservation implies both nature conservation and sustainable development (Raharimahefa, 2012).

According to Farsani et al., (2010), geoparks can support economic development since new job opportunities and new economic activities can be developed in regions with geoparks. These new jobs and new activities can increase the sources of local income. Moreover, geoparks can be seen as examples of sustainable development at the local level (Farsani et al., 2010).

In Romania, there are two geoparks officially designated, namely the Mehedinti Plateau Geopark and the Hateg Dinosaurus Geopark. The overall aim of geoparks is to achieve sustainable socio-economic development (Stoleriu, 2014).

We have mentioned above about Zânei Hill, which has been proposed as geopark (Popa et al., 2010) due to the numerous Jurassic fossils that may be found there. Popa et al., (2010) consider that having a geopark at the Zânei Hill will enhance the environmental protection and will represent a chance for the economic development of Anina town.

Based on numerous studies in different parts of the world, we may highlight that a geopark developed in Anina Mountains can bring a large range of benefits in the educational field, in environmental protection, in geotourism and finally in the economic aspects of human communities in this region. Zânei Hill is close to Miniș Gorges, Plopa Cave, and Ponor Cave, meaning that a geopark may be easily linked to other great geomorphosites within this region. Moreover, since Plopa Cave is the place where Europe's earliest modern humans' bones were discovered (Zilhão et al., 2007; Rougier et al., 2007), this geosite may be promoted into a sustainable way in order to enhance tourism activities and scientific studies. Consequently, a geotouristic itinerary that may include this proposed geopark can be developed in order to include different types of geosites.

RESULTS AND DISCUSSIONS

The presence of geosites in Anina Mountains may improve natural features protection and economic development of this region.

Even if most of the people consider that stones, rocks, and landscapes can't bring any added value to the communities living in regions rich in geodiversity, in fact, these natural features represent our history and the evolution of natural environment, which means that we have access to a very rich heritage. Consequently, geotourism has become more important every day in numerous countries around the world due to the important benefits, such as economic, social, cultural and educational (Abdel Maksoud and Hussien, 2016).

Based on Abdel Maksoud and Hussien (2016) statement, local people from Anina Mountains may benefit from the presence of such a rich geological and geomorphological heritage in order to improve their social, cultural, educational and economic aspects.

Because geodiveristy and geomorphosites can promote geotourism, it is important to highlight the subdomains and activities which play important roles in promoting education, environmental protection, and economic development through geodiversity (Figure 9).

According to Lukic et al., (2016), learning about geoheritage and geodiversity, students can enrich their knowledge in sustainable development. Consequently, awareness regarding preserving geodiversity will increase.

The educational role may be based on Geography as a fundamental domain for students. Together with Geography, Ecological Education is another field of study that represents a must for young people to understand the role of geodiversity for their communities and for the entire world. Of course, in Geography and Ecological Education the theoretical part is not enough since fieldwork is the part that consolidates the theory achieved during the class hours.

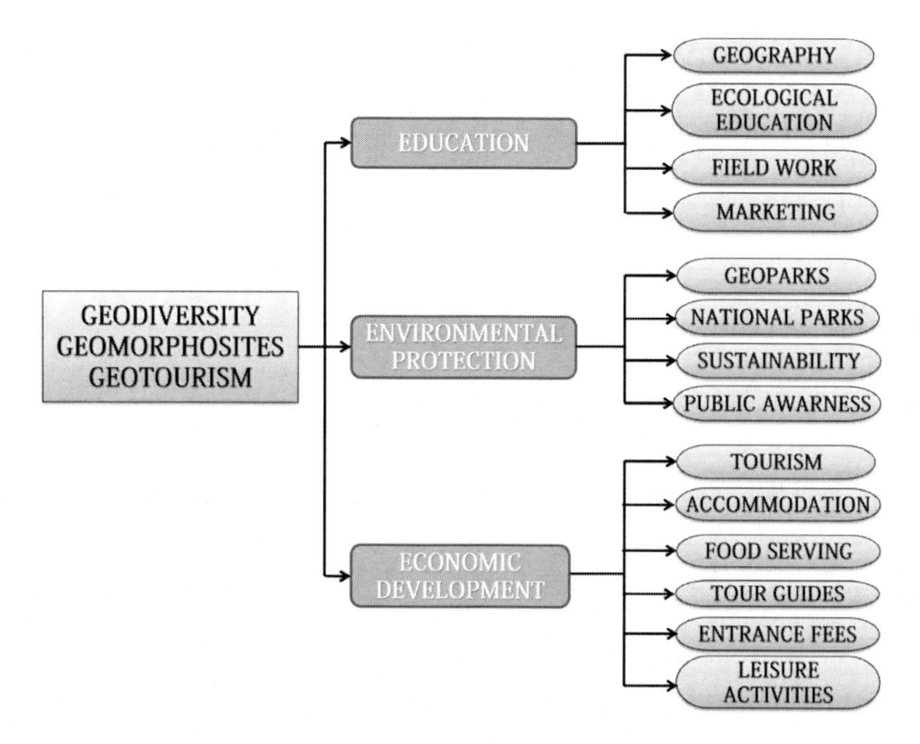

Figure 9. Main roles of geodiversity/geomorphosites/geotourism in education, environmental protection and economic development.

In order to promote geodiversity, we consider that gaining knowledge in the field of marketing is essential. Consequently, each community that intends to value the geodiversity of their surrounding areas, they should learn marketing. By learning marketing, each community may promote the geodiversity in a feasible way and attract numerous investors and tourists.

Geomorphosites promotion and geotourism may represent sustainable methods to provide a good scientific formation to different levels of audience and teach the audience regarding the evolution of different landscapes. In order to ensure this scientific formation, theoretical lessons, laboratory activities, and fieldwork trips are necessary (Bollati et al., 2011).

Going further with another role of geodiversity, environmental protection may be achieved through geoparks, national parks, public awareness, and sustainability. Anina Mountains include already two national parks, which represent an important support for the role of environmental protection supported by geodiversity. Moreover, a geopark at Zânei Hill is already proposed (Popa et al., 2010) and if this plan becomes reality, then the new geopark would help for a better environmental protection.

Public awareness should be achieved by education and different activities those should help local communities understand the benefits of having an ecologic attitude towards the environment. Through national parks, geoparks and public awareness, the idea of sustainability is strongly supported by the people living in the communities of Anina Mountains.

If geodiversity roles in education and environmental protection are successfully completed, then the third role of geodiversity, namely economic development, would be much easier to implement. Geodiversity may lead to economic development through tourism, which includes accommodation, leisure activities, food serving, entrances fee and tour guides. Accommodation, food serving, and tour guides can bring important income for the local population since tourists need a place to stay and to eat. Moreover, many local people may earn money as tour guides, since local people know very well the region and they may guide the visitors to visit the most beautiful places and the most representative geosites. Of course, entrances fee should be added as an important source of income for local communities. Finally, leisure activities those may be linked to different geosites can also represent an important source of income for local communities.

Numerous threats may put in danger the features that give a high level of geodiversity, such as urbanization, changes in land use, tourism activities or irresponsible fossil and mineral collecting (Hjort et al., 2015). On the other hand, the threats those may affect the geoheritage are divided by Raharimahefa (2012) into natural threats and threats caused by human activities.

The highest threats towards geodiversity are due to human activities and are caused by planning development and land use changes. The consequences of these human activities include geosites damaging, fragment the interest towards these geosites and impair accessibility and visibility (Erhartič and Zorn, 2012).

Raharimahefa (2012) mentions that there are some barriers those may affect geoconservation, such as deforestation, illegal logging, poaching and political decision to keep the local population living in or in the proximities of geosites in poverty.

In order to overcome these threats those may put in danger geosites, it is extremely important to ensure a legal framework that may provide protection for geosites and landscape. Anina Mountains benefits from the presence of numerous nature reserves and two national parks which are able to ensure a certain level of protection.

Unfortunately, there are some threats that can put in danger the geosites within this region. The most important threats observed during field applications in Anina Mountains include deforestation, mineral collecting, caves vandalizing and waste disposal in nature. Deforestation and illegal logging generate rapid runoff, soil loss and speleothems destruction due to heavy trucks carrying logs on forest roads above caves (such as for example above Buhui Cave and Cuptoare Cave), caves vandalizing include actions like breaking speleothems and caves' walls writing, while mineral collecting generates loss of attractions of paleontological sites due to the loss of the elements of attraction.

Some of these threats are related to tourism activities, but some of them are not. Consequently, by improving geotourism and increasing the number of visitors, threats like deforestation and waste disposal in nature may be reduced due to an increased visibility of this region in mass media at local, national or even international level.

By promoting geosites and geotourism, and developing the socio-economical life of local communities in Anina Mountains, another barrier that may affect geoconservation (Raharimahefa, 2012) may be solved, namely the poverty of the local population. Increasing the attraction and incomes of each community in Anina Mountains, local people may benefit from higher earnings and the improvement of their living conditions.

PROPOSALS AND SUGGESTIONS

We consider that geomorphosites can represent the greatest fortune of the people living in the Anina Mountains. These geomorphosites can attract numerous tourists and can generate high rates of income. Moreover, through geotourism, numerous jobs may become available and the unemployment rate may decrease considerably. By becoming an attractive tourist region at national and international scale, Anina Mountains can overcome the numerous economic and social issues those were identified during the field visits.

In order to value these geosites and bring economic development in the communities living in Anina Mountains, it is important to keep in mind that the environment is very fragile, especially the karst landscape. Consequently, protecting the environment should be a pillar of valuing these geomorphosites.

Satmari (2009) considers that we expect today ecological acquaintance to a people that have never received an ecological education. Based on this lack of ecological education, geodiversity may be promoted as a great tool for environmental protection education and economic progress.

The lack of knowledge and lack of information received by the local population regarding the high richness of these places may be solved by information and awareness campaigns regarding the value of karst landscapes in Anina Mountains.

Education is another solution to overcome lack of knowledge and awareness among the local population. Due to this, our suggestion is to include in the table of disciplines of local schools at least one course per week regarding geoconservation or geoheritage. By doing this, starting from their childhood the upcoming adults of these communities will understand the roles and the benefits of geosites to this region. Consequently, in the near future, these communities will not have to face issues like poverty and depopulation.

In the near future, we intend to apply a questionnaire among both local people and tourists/potential tourists regarding their perception about geosites within Anina Mountains. Moreover, as geographers and experts in the tourism field, we intend to organize several presentations for local communities to inform them about the importance of geological sites and how these geosites can bring economic progress.

CONCLUSION

After a deep research in the field and a detailed literature review, the present study's conclusions bring into public awareness the positive role of geodiversity in nature conservation, education and socio-economic development in Anina Mountains, Romania.

The region of Anina Mountains benefits from the great advantage of numerous and a high density of geosites. Another plus for this region is that most of these geosites are located within two national parks. By benefiting from these strong aspects, the communities that are part of this region may gain economic development and better living conditions for the largest part of the population.

If in the past nature ensured the economic development to the most of the communities within Anina Mountains through coal resources, nowadays geomorphosites can bring again the shine for these communities. Promoting geosites and geotourism, local communities can benefit from better education, a high level of environmental protection and a strong economic development. All these together can ensure a sustainable development of the entire region, sustainable development being a desideratum of each human community in the last decades.

According to Abdel Maksoud and Hussien (2016), geotourism is among the most important economic development factor due to its role in employment opportunities, increase in gross domestic product, enlarging the sources of income for local populations and attracting numerous investors. Moreover, geotourism can contribute to reviving traditional culture in local communities.

A strong local involvement, protecting the environment, conserving the original and remarkable geological features, and organizing activities to communicate geo-scientific knowledge represent the minim requirements for the education, environmental protection and economic development roles brought by geomorphosites and geodiversity into Anina Mountains.

To conclude, we may say that, after numerous field applications, discussions with people living in communities within Anina Mountains, analyzing other regions around the world having a rich geodiversity and reading numerous studies regarding roles that geodiversity can have in different parts of the world, the geodiversity of Anina Mountains may represent the greatest fortune of people living in communities in this region and this fortune should be capitalized accordingly.

REFERENCES

Abdel Maksoud, K. M., Hussien, M. G. (2016). Geotourism in Egypt and its Economic and Culture Impact. *Arabian Journal of Earth Sciences*, Vol. 3, Issue 1: 1-13.

Alexandrowicz, Z., Kozlowski, S. (1999). From selected geosites to geodiversity conservation – Polish example of modern framework. In: Barretino, D., Vallejo, M., Gallego, E. (Eds.). *Towards the Balanced Management and Conservation of the Geological Heritage in the New Millenium*, pp. 40-44.

Artugyan, L. (2014). Geomorphosites as a Valuable Resource for Tourism Development in a Deprived Area. The Case Study of Anina Karstic Region (Banat Mountains, Romania). *Analele Universităţii din Oradea – Seria Geografie*, Year XXIV, no. 2/2014, 89-100.

Artugyan, L. (2017). Geomorphosites Assessment in Karst Terrains: Anina Karst Region (Banat Mountains, Romania). *Geoheritage*, 9(2), pp. 153-162, DOI:10.1007/s12371-016-0188-x.

Bollati, I., Pelfini, M., Pellegrini, L., Bazzi, A., Duci, G. (2011). Active geomorphosites and educational application: an itinerary along Trebbia River (Northern Apennines, Italy). In: Reynard E., Laigre L. et Kramar N. (Eds). *Les géosciences au service de la société. Actes du colloque en l'honneur du Professeur Michel Marthaler*, 24-26 juin 2010, Lausanne (Géovisions no. 37). Institut de géographie, Université de

Lausanne, [*Geoscience at the service of society. Proceedings of the conference in honor of Professor Michel Marthaler*, 24-26 June 2010, Lausanne (Géovisions 37). Institute of Geography, University of Lausanne], pp. 221-233.

Bucur, I. I. (1997). *Formaţiunile mezozoice din zona Reşiţa-Moldova Nouă (Munţii Aninei şi estul Munţilor Locvei)*. Editura Presa Universitară Clujeană, Cluj-Napoca, 214 p. [*Mesosoic Formations in Reșița-Moldova Nouă Zone (Anina Mountains and the east of Locvei Mountains)*. Presa Universitară Clujeană Publishing House, Cluj-Napoca, 214 p.]

Brilha, J. (2016). Inventory and Quantitative Assessment of Geosites and Geodiversity Sites: a Review. *Geoheritage*, 8:119–134, DOI 10.1007/s12371-014-0139-3.

Chakrabarty, P., Mandal, R. (2018). Geotourism Mapping for Sustainability: A Basin Oriented Approach. *GeoJournal of Tourism and Geosites*, Year XI, no. 1, vol. 21, p.174-185.

Comănescu, L., Dobre, R. (2009). Inventorying, evaluating and tourism valuating the geomorphosites from the central sector of The Ceahlău National Park. *GeoJournal of Tourism and Geosites*, 3(1): 86–96, Year II.

Comănescu, L., Nedelea, A. (2010). Analysis of some representative geomorphosites in the Bucegi Mountains: between scientific evaluation and tourist perception. *Area*, 42(4):406–416, doi:10.1111/j.1475-4762.2010.00937.

Comănescu, L., Nedelea, A., Dobre, R. (2012) The evaluation of geomorphosites from the Ponoare Protected Area. *Forum Geografic, Studii și Cercetări de Geografie și Protecția Mediului*, XI(1):54–61, doi:10.5775/fg.2067-4635.2012.037.i.

Comănescu, L., Nedelea, A., Dobre, R. (2013) The geotouristic map—between theory and practical use. Case study the central sector of the Bucegi Mountains (Romania). *GeoJournal of Tourism and Geosites*, 11(1):16–22, Year VI.

Comănescu, L., Nedelea, A., Stănoiu, G. (2017). Geomorphosites and geotourism in Bucharest City Center (Romania). *Quaestiones Geographicae*, 36(3), 51-61.

Comer, P. J., Pressey, R. L., Hunter, M. L. Jr, Schloss, C. A., Buttrick, S. C., Heller, N. E., Tirpak, J. M., Faith, D. P., Cross, M. S., Shaffer, M. L. (2015). Incorporating geodiversity into conservation decisions. *Conservation Biology*, 29, 692–701.

Coratza, P., Galve, J. P., Soldati, M., Tonelli, C. (2012). Recognition and assessment of sinkholes as geosites: lessons from the Island of Gozo (Malta). *Quaestiones Geographicae*, 31(1):25–35. doi:10.2478/ v10117-012-0006-8.

Crişan, H. F., Irimuş, I. A., Peteley, A., Balint-Balint, L., Mara, V. (2015). Karst Geomorphosites from the Giurgeu Mountains (Romania). 15th International Multidisciplinary Scientific GeoConference SGEM 2015, *SGEM2015 Conference Proceedings, Book 5*, Vol. 2, 279-286 pp., DOI: 10.5593/SGEM2015/B52/S20.037.

Dowling, R. K. (2011). Geotourism's Global Growth. *Geoheritage*, 3:1-13.

Dowling, R. K. (2013). Global Geotourism – An Emerging Form of Sustainable Tourism. *Czech Journal of Tourism*, 02 / 2013, pp. 59-79.

Erhartič, B. (2010). Geomorphosite assessment. *Acta Geographica Slovenica*, 50–2:295–319.

Erhartič, B., Zorn, M. (2012). Geodiversity and Geomorphosite Research in Slovenia. *Geografski Vestnik*, 84-1, 51–63.

Farsani, N. T., Coelho, C., Costa, C. (2010). Geotourism and Geoparks as Novel Strategies for Socio-economic Development in Rural Areas. *International Journal of Tourism Research*, Published online in Wiley InterScience.

Farsani, N., Coelho, C., Costa, C., (2011). Geotourism and Geoparks as Gateways to Socio-cultural Sustainability in Qeshm Rural Areas, Iran, *Asia Pacific Journal of Tourism Research*, Vol. 17, No. 1, 30-48.

Feuillet, T., Sourp, E. (2011). Geomorphological heritage of the Pyrenees National Park (France): assessment, clustering, and promotion of geomorphosites. *Geoheritage*, 3:151–162. doi:10.1007/s12371-010-0020-y.

Forleo, M. B., Giannelli, A., Giaccio, V., Palmieri, N., Mastronardi, L. (2017). Geosites and Parks for the Sustainable Development of Inner Areas: The Matese Mountain (Italy). *GeoJournal of Tourism and Geosites*, Year X, no. 2, vol. 20, p. 231-242.

Gavrilă I. G., Man, T., Surdeanu, V. (2011). Geomorphological heritage assessement using GIS analyses for geotourism development in Măcin Mountains, Dobrogea, Romania. *GeoJournal of Tourism and Geosites*, IV (2): 198–205.

Gavrilă, I. G., Anghel, T. (2013). Geomorphosites inventory in the Măcin Mountains (South-Eastern Romania). *GeoJournal of Tourism and Geosites*, 11(1):42–53, Year VI.

Ghiraldi, L., Coratza, P., De Biaggi, E., Giardino, M., Marchetti, M., Perotti, L. (2009). Development and usage of Geosites: new results from research and conservation activities in the Piemonte Region (Italy). *Studia Universitatis Babeş-Bolyai - Geologia*, 54(2), 23-26.

Goran, C. (1982). *Catalogul sistematic al peşterilor din România*, Inst. Speol., Fed. Rom. Turism-Alpinism, Com. Centr. Speol. Sport., Bucureşti, 496 p. [*Systematic catalogue of caves in Romania*, Speleological Institute, Romanian Federation of Tourism-Alpinism, Buchrest, 496 p.]

Gordon, J. E., Barron, H. F. (2012). Valuing geodiversity and geoconservation: developing a more strategic ecosystem approach. *Scottish Geographical Journal*, 128, pp. 278-297.

Gray, M. (2013). *Geodiversity: Valuing and conserving abiotic nature*. 2nd edition. Wiley-Blackwell, Chichester, United Kingdom.

Gray, M., Gordon, J. E., Brown, E. J. (2013). Geodiversity and the ecosystem approach: the contribution of geoscience in delivering integrated environmental management. *Proceedings of the Geologists' Association*, 124:659–673.

Henriques, M. H., Tomaz, C., Sa, A. A. (2012). The Arouca Geopark (Portugal) as an educational resource: A case study. *Episodes*, Vol. 35, no. 4, pp. 481-488.

Hjort, J., Gordon, J. E., Gray, M., Hunter Jr., M. L. (2015). Why geodiversity matters in valuing nature's stage. *Conservation Biology*, Volume 29, No. 3, 630–639.

Hose, T. A. (2007). *Geotourism in Almeria Province, Southeast Spain. Tourism*, 55(3): 259–276.

Hoyos, M., Soler, V., Canaveras, J. C., Sánchez-Moral, S., Sanz-Rubio, E. (1998). Microclimatic characterization of a karst cave: human impact on microenvironmental parameters of a prehistoric rock art cave (Candamo Cave, northern Spain). *Environmental Geology*, 33(4), 231–242.

Iamandei, M. I. (2017). The Main Karstic Geomorphosites with High Touristic Value in Mehedinți Plateau. *International Journal of Academic Research in Environment and Geography*, Vol. 4, No. 1, pp. 65-76.

Ilinca, V., Comănescu, L. (2011). Aspects concerning some of the geomorphosites with tourist value from Vâlcea County (Romania). *GeoJournal of Tourism and Geosites*, 1(7): 22-32, Year IV.

Kubalíková, L. (2013). Geomorphosite assessment for geotourism purposes. *Czech Journal of Tourism*, 2(2):80–104. doi:10.2478/cjot-2013-0005.

Kubalíková, L., Kirchner, K. (2015). Geosite and geomorphosite assessment as a tool for geoconservation and geotourism purposes: a case study from Vizovická Vrchovina highland (eastern part of the Czech Republic). *Geoheritage*. doi:10.1007/s12371-015-0143-2.

Lukic, D., Andjelkovic, S., Dedjanski, V. (2016). Geodiversity and geoheritage in Geography teaching for the purpose of improving students' competencies in education for sustainable development. *Forum geografic. Studii și cercetări de geografie și protecția mediului*, Vol. XV, Issue 2, pp. 210-217, http://dx.doi.org/10.5775/fg.2067-4635.2016.348.d.

Mateescu, F. (1961). Influențe structurale în relieful Munților Carașului. *Probleme de geografie*, vol. VIII, Institutul de Geologie și Geografie, București, pp. 205–219. [Structural influences of the relief of Caraș

Mountains. *Geographical problems*, vol. VIII, The Institute of Geology and Geography, Bucharest, pp. 205-219].

Mc Keever, P., Zouros, N. (2005). Geoparks: Celebrating Earth heritage, sustaining local communities, *Episodes*, v. 28, no 4, pp. 274-278.

Miccadei, E., Sammarone, L., Piacentini, T., D'Amico, D., Mancinelli, V. (2014). Geotourism in the Abruzzo, Lazio and Molise National Park (Central Italy): the example of Mount Greco and Chiarano Valley. *GeoJournal of Tourism and Geosites*, 13(1):38–51, Year VII.

Necheş I. M. (2013). From geomorphosite evaluation to geotourism interpretation. Case study: the Sphinx of Romania's Southern Carpathians. *GeoJournal of Tourism and Geosites*, 12(2):145–162, Year VI.

Necheş I. M., Erdeli, G. (2015). Geolandscapes and Geotourism: Integrating Nature and Culture in the Bucegi Mountains of Romania. *Landscape Research*, 40:4, 486-509, DOI: 10.1080/01426397.2014.939616.

Onac, B. (2000). *Geologia regiunilor carstice*. Universitatea "Babes-Bolyai" Cluj-Napoca, Institutul de Speologie "Emil Racoviță" Cluj-Napoca, 399 p. [*Geology of karst region*, "Babes-Bolyai" University Cluj-Napoca, "Emil Racoviță" Speleological Institute Cluj-Napoca, 399 p.].

Orăşeanu, I., Iurkiewicz, A. (2010). *Karst hydrogeology of Romania*. Ed. Federaţia Română de Speologie, Oradea.

Orghidan, T. (1972). The fiftieth anniversary of the first speleological institute of the World, *AAPG Bulletin/International Journal of Speleology*, Vol. 4, Issue 1, p. 1-7.

Panizza, M. (2009). The geomorphodiversity of the Dolomites (Italy): A key of geoheritage assessment. *Geoheritage*, 1:33–42. doi:10.1007/s12371-009-0003-z.

Pelfini, M., Bollati, I. (2014). Landforms and Geomorphosites Ongoing Changes: Concepts and Implications for Geoheritage Promotion. *Quaestiones Geographicae*, 33(1), pp.131-143.

Pereira, P., Pereira, D. (2010). Methodological guidelines for geomorphosite assessment. *Géomorphologie: relief, processus, environnement*, 2, 215–222.

Popa, M. E., Meller, B. (2009). Review of Jurassic Plants from the Anina (Steierdorf) Coal Mining Area, South Carpathians, in the Collections of the Geological Survey of Austria. *Jahrbuchder Geologischen Bundesanstalt*, 149 (4), 487–498.

Popa, M. E., Kedzior, A., Fodolică, V. (2010). The Anina Geopark: Preserving the Geological Heritage of the South Carpathians. *Rev. Roum. Géologie*, 53–54, 109–113.

Pralong, J. P. (2005). A method for assessing tourist potential and use of geomorphological sites. *Géomorphologie: relief, processus, environnement*, 3, 189–196.

Purice, C., Romanescu, Gh., Romanescu, G. (2013). The Protection of the Geomorphosites Within the Măcin Mountains National Park (Romania) and Their Touristic Importance. *International Journal of Conservation Science*, Vol. 4, Issue 3, 373-383.

Raharimahefa, T. (2012). Geoconservation and geodiversity for sustainable development in Madagascar. *Madagascar Conservation & Development*, Vol. 7, Issue 3, pp. 126-134.

Răileanu, Gr., Năstăseanu, S., Boldur, C. (1964). Sedimentarul paleozoic și mezozoic al Domeniului getic din partea sudvestică a Carpaților Meridionali. *Anuarul Comitetului Geologic*, XXXIV, București, 5–58. [Palaeozoic and Mesozoic sedimentary of Getic Nappe from the south-western part of Southern Carpathians. *The Year-Book of Geological Committee,* XXXIV, Bucharest, 5-58].

Rougier, H., Milota, S., Rodrigo, R., Gherase, M., Sarcină, L., Molclovan, O., Zilhão, J., Constantin, S., Franciscus, R. G., Zollikofer, C. P. E., de León, M. P., Trinkaus, E. (2007). Peştera cu Oase 2 and the cranial morphology of early modern Europeans. *Proceedings of the National Academy of Sciences USA*, 104, pp. 1165-1170.

Safarabadi, A., Shahzeidi, S. S. (2018). Tourism Silence in Geomorphosites: A Case Study of Ali-Sadr Cave (Hamadan, Iran). *GeoJournal of Tourism and Geosites*, Year XI, no. 1, vol. 21, p.49-60.

Satmari, A. (2009). *Analiza geosistemică a spaţiului urban şi periurban Anina*. Ed. Eurobit, Timişoara, 225 p. [*Geosystemic analysis of urban and periurban space in Anina*. Eurobit Publishing House, Timișoara, 225 p.].

Sencu, V. (1964). Cercetări asupra carstului din partea sudică a localităţii Anina (Banat). Peşterile din bazinele pâraielor Steierdorf şi Ponor. *Studii și Cercetări de Geologie, Geofizică și Geografie*, 11, 140–162. [Research on the karst terrain in the southern part of Anina (Banat). Caves in the Steierdorf and Ponor creeks' watersheds. *Studies and Research of Geology, Geophysics and Geography*, 11, 140-162].

Sencu, V. (1978). *Munţii Aninei*, Editura Sport-Turism, Bucureşti, 86 p. [*Anina Mountains*, Sport-Tourism Publishing House, Bucharest, 86 p.].

Serrano, E., González-Trueba, J. J. (2005). Assessment of geomorphosites in natural protected areas: the Picos de Europa National Park (Spain). *Géomorphologie: Relief Processus Environment*, 3:197–208.

Stoleriu, O. M. (2014). National approaches to geotourism and geoparks in Romania. *14th International Multidisciplinary Scientific Geo Conference SGEM 2014 - Ecology and Environmental Protection*.

Trinkaus, E., Milota, Ş., Rodrigo, R., Gherase, M., Moldovan, O. (2003a). Early modern human cranial remains from the Peştera cu Oase, Romania. *Journal of Human Evolution*, 45, 245–253.

Trinkaus, E., Moldovan, O., Milota, Ş., Bîlgăr, A., Sarcină, L., Athreya, S., Bailey, S. E., Rodrigo, R., Gherase, M., Higham, T., Bronk Ramsey, C., Van der Plicht, J. (2003b). An early modern human from the Peştera cu Oase, Romania. *Proceedings of the National Academy of Sciences USA*, 100, 11231–11236.

Zgłobicki, W., Baran-Zgłobicka, B. (2013). Geomorphological heritage as a tourist attraction. A case study in Lubelskie Province, SE Poland. *Geoheritage*, 5:137–149. doi:10.1007/s12371-013-0076-6.

Zhyrnov, P. (2015). Geomorphosite Assessment Method of Karst Landscapes by Considering the Geomorphological Factors. *Geomorphologia Slovaca et Bohemica*, 2, pp. 7-19.

Zilhão, J., Trinkaus, E., Constantin, S., Milota, S., Gherase, M., Sarcină, L., Danciu, A. Rougier, H., Quiles, J., Rodrigo, R. (2007). The Pestera cu Oase people, Europe's earliest modern humans. In Mellars, P., Boyle, K., Bar-Yosef, O., Stringer, C. (Eds.). *Rethinking the Human Revolution,* McDonald Institute, Cambridge, pp.249-262.

Zouros, N. (2010). Geodiversity and Sustainable Development: Geoparks - A New Challenge for Research and Education in Earth Sciences. *Bulletin of the Geological Society of Greece. Proceedings of the 12th International Congress*, Patras, May, 2010.

Biographical Sketch

Laurenţiu Artugyan

Affiliation: non-affiliated, Independent researcher, freelancer science writer

Education:

2012 – 2015: Doctorate

Thesis title: INTEGRATED KARST GEOMORPHOLOGY STUDY IN THE ANINA KARST AREA (BANAT MOUNTAINS)

West University of Timisoara, Romania, Faculty of Chemistry-Biology-Geography, Department of Geography, Doctoral School „Environment and Sustainable Development"

2010 – 2012: Master

West University of Timisoara, Romania, Faculty of Chemistry-Biology-Geography, Department of Geography, Geographical Informational Systems (GIS) Specialization

2007 – 2010: Bachelor

West University of Timisoara, Romania, Faculty of Chemistry-Biology-Geography, Department of Geography, Geography of Tourism Specialization

Training activities:

- GISLERS Summer School "GISLERS - Bridging Geographic Information Science, Landscape Ecology and Remote Sensing for Landscape Analysis and landscape planning," 27.06.2011–08.07.2011, University of Salzburg, Centre for Geoinformatics (Z_GIS) (Salzburg, Austria).
- Geoinformatics Forum (GI_Forum), Salzburg University, Austria, 05-08.07.2011 during GISLERS Summer School "GISLERS - Bridging Geographic Information Science, Landscape Ecology and Remote Sensing for Landscape Analysis and landscape planning"
- Specialization scholarship in Geographical Informational Systems (CEEPUS II Program): 03.10.2011–31.10.2011, University of Salzburg, Centre for Geoinformatics (Z_GIS) (Salzburg, Austria)
- Grantee of "Cross-border network for advanced training and research in environmental protection," IPA Cross-Border Cooperation Programme "Romania-Serbia" (ROSNET) as student at Department of Geography, West University Timisoara: april 2011 - august 2012.
- Grantee of "Cross Border Doctoral Programs Consortium, HURO/1001/184/2.3.1" as PhD student at the Department of Geography, West University Timisoara; Octomber 2012 - September 2013.
- Specialization scholarship in Geographical Informational Systems (CEEPUS III Program): 03.03.2014–30.04.2014, University of Zagreb, Department of Geodesy (Croatia).
- Interdisciplinary Workshop: Post-Industrial Regeneration in Anina, 27th of July - 3rd of August 2014, Anina, Romania.
- "HURO EnviArch - Geophyiscal applications in archaeology and environmental science" Summer School; 22-25.09.2014, Timisoara, West University Timisoara, Department of Geography (Timisoara, Romania)
- Specialization scholarship in Geographical Informational Systems (CEEPUS III Program): 02.03.2015–30.04.2015, Palacký

University, Olomouc, Department of Geoinformatics (Czech Republic).

- Grantee of the Grant POSDRU/159/1.5/S/133391"Doctoral and Post-doctoral programs of excellence for highly qualified human resources training for research in the field of Life sciences, Environment and Earth Science" as PhD student at the Department of Geography, West University Timisoara; May 2014- December 2015.

Research and Professional Experience:

- Geomorphology
- Karst Geomorphology
- Geographic Information System (GIS)
- Remote Sensing (RS)
- Cartography and Digital Mapping
- Speleology
- Tourism (Ecotourism, Geotourism)
- Environmental Protection

2016-2017: Teacher of Geography at "Socrates" High-School in Timişoara, 5th – 8th Grades

2012-2015: Teaching Assistant in Cartography, Geographic Information System (GIS) and field applications at West University of Timisoara, Romania, Faculty of Chemistry-Biology-Geography, Department of Geography

Publications from the Last 3 Years:

Artugyan, L., Ardelean, A. C., Urdea, P. (2015). Characterization of Karst Terrain Using Geophysical Methods Based on Sinkhole Analysis: A Case Study of Anina Karstic Region (Banat Mountains, Romania); NCKRI Symposium 5, *Proceedings of the 14th Multidisciplinary*

Conference on Sinkholes and the Engineering and Environmental Impacts of Karst, 387-397. doi: 10.5038/9780991000951.1044.

Artugyan, L. (2015). Using GIS for Caves Modelling and Analysis. The Study Case of Anina Mining Area (Banat Mountains, Romania). *Analele Universităţii din Oradea – Seria Geografie*, Year XXV, no. 2/2015 (December), pp. 261-268.

Artugyan, L., Urdea, P. (2016). Using Digital Elevation Model (Dem) in Karst Terrain Analysis. Study Case: Anina Mining Area (Banat Mountains, Romania). *Carpathian Journal of Earth and Environmental Sciences*, Vol. 11, No. 1, p. 55-64.

Artugyan, L. (2017). Geomorphosites Assessment in Karst Terrains: Anina Karst Region (Banat Mountains, Romania), *Geoheritage*, 9, 153–162, DOI 10.1007/s12371-016-0188-x.

In: Romania
Editor: Sophie Clarke
ISBN: 978-1-53614-590-8
© 2018 Nova Science Publishers, Inc.

Chapter 2

LOOKING TOWARDS GREEN ENERGY: SOLAR CELLS, E-MOTION AND BUILDINGS IN ROMANIA

Mihaiela Iliescu[1,*], Luige Vlădăreanu[1], Marius Pandelea[1], Adrian Mărgean[2] and Alexandru Rogojinaru[3]

[1]Department of Mechatronics and Robotics,
Institute of Solid Mechanics of Romanian Academy,
Bucharest, Romania
[2]TOP AMBIENT SRL, Romanian SME
[3]E-MOTION ELECTRIC, Romanian SME

ABSTRACT

In this chapter we (authors) evidence main aspects of the interest in "green" (energy, motion/mobility, building/construction) – from the authorities and, maybe most important, from the inhabitants of Romania, at the end of second decade of XXI centrury.

[*] Corresponding Author Email: iliescumihaiela7@gmail.com.

First, there should be mentioned the interest in producing green energy, especially renewable one, solar energy. There are a lot of funds allocated to scientifc research and, consequently, to its applied results with benefits and commercial potential. Thus, an innovative equipment designed and prototyped so as to obtain solar cells (based on perovskite) with PCE (Power conversion efficiency) not less than 15%, is presented.

Another aspect of Romania's green trend is that of electric e-motion. It is about the population interest in buying and, further, using electric bikes, hybrid or, completely, electric cars and, consequently, SMEs involvement in installing e-charging stations – all over countryside. For the moment, the focus is on public parking (in hypermarkets, malls) and on main fuel stations of the main providers (OMV, Rompetrol, Petrom, etc.).

Last, but not least, in Romania there is an increasing interest in building with low pollution, high efficiency and environmental friendly. LGS (Light Gauge Steel) load bearing systems are the ones used in building houses, industrial halls, silos and farms, so that they are ecological and sustainable. Some aspects of scientific research, as well as its application and benefits in manufacturing LGS profiles, when building "metallic" houses, are evidenced.

Bottom line, nowadays Romania is looking towards green – in the terms of environmental friendly, efficiency, user friendly and, why not, less expensive, even on long term.

1. INTRODUCTION

The dramatic and, many times, unexpected climatic changes, as well as nowadays reality of conventional energy resources (coal, oil, water) depletion, focus the attention of humanity on friendly environmental products and technlogies, as well as on exploitation and use of non-conventional, renewable energy resources (sun, wind).

For exemaple, it is mentioned in [1] that on September, 2017, almost 50% of electric energy in Romania was generated by renewable energy resources, the wind power generating about one third (30.73%) of national production, at the power of 2,258 MW. According to the same source, nuclear energy was ranked 3, with 1,385 MW (19%); photovoltaic energy generated into the system 487 MW, (6,63%) and biomass generated 45 MW (0,61%) out of the total.

In order to reduce greenhouse gas emissions [2], Romanian Government launched (on March 26, 2018) for financing the program "Rabla Plus", for the period 2017 – 2019. This program is aimed to encourage population and institutions to diminish CO and CO_2 emissions by using new, energy efficient cars, specially focusing on hybrid and electric cars. In fact, for one new electric car, one gets approximately 10,000 euro as governmental subvention.

Sales of eco-cars have been growing [3], [4] by 64.2% in the first three months of 2018, when compared to the same period of year 2017, up to 661 units, according to Automotive Manufacturers and Importers Association (APIA). While January- March, 2018, the green cars sales represent 2.2%, while for the same period of 2017, the percentage was 1.7%. In March, 2018, there have been sold 269 electric and hybrid cars which stands for an 35.17% increase, compared to February, 2018, when the number of sold cars was 199. On the Romanian market, the price offer [5] for electric cars varies in between 25,838 and 39,151 euro. Considering the governmental subvention it is estimated a high increase of electric/hybrid cars to be driven on Romanian highways, boulevards and streets (see Figure 1).

Figure 1. Sales of electric and hybrid cars have known spectacular increase in Romania [3].

Figure 2. Light Gauge Steel constructions [7].

Construction market in 2017 and, specially, in 2018 has been continuous increasing, for both offices and residential. Buildings on Light Gauge Steel, LGS, profiles have been proved to be an innovative solution for sustainability, ecological and efficient constructions, with spectacular resistance to earthquakes, generically called "eco-buildings" (see Figure 2).

Some of LGS constructions benefits are as follows: does not deplete forests and is 100% recyclable; highest strength-to-weight ratio of any building material; cleaner building site with less rubble to remove from site; high safety in earthquake.

2. Printer for Perovskite Solar Cells

The context of the development of solar cells and, in particular, those with perovskites, is evoked in [8]. Using photovoltaic cells to convert solar energy is, by far, the cleanest method to generate electricity. Currently, the market for photovoltaic cells is dominated by those based on Crystalline Si (about 89% of the market) and on thin films (about 11% of the market, mainly using CdTe and GIGS) [9]. Hybrid solar cells such as those based on sensitive pigments are now a very small percentage of the market due to their low efficiency. Therefore, efficient use of free solar energy, minimizing costs and developing large-scale applications is currently a subject of great interest. One of the main challenges of the research community is the development of cheaper integrated materials, devices and systems that are capable of converting solar energy directly into electricity.

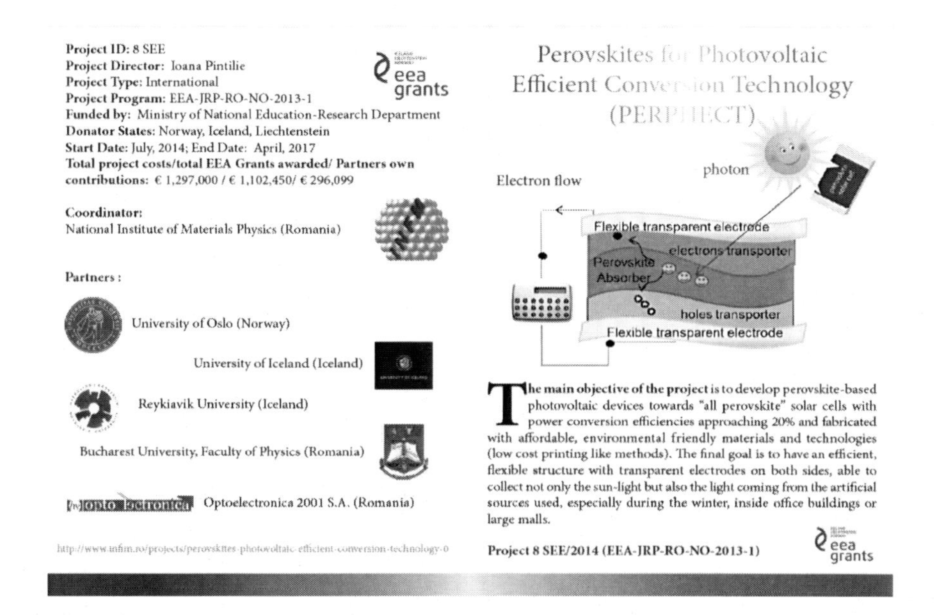

Figure 3. "PERPHECT" project leaflet [11].

The standard perovskite solar cell is manufactured on a glass support (rigid) coated with a transparent oxide (FTO or ITO) over which there are successively deposited: compact layer and a mesoporous TiO2 which acts as an electron transporting material; light absorber which is a halogen perovskite (CH3NH3PbI3), abbreviated as MAPI; hollow conveyor (spiro-OMeTAD); Ag or Au back electrode.

Based on the sudden and unexpected progress reported in autumn 2013 on solar cells using halogenated perovskite compounds as a photon absorber, research teams from the National Institute of Materials Physics (NIMP), University of Oslo, University of Iceland, Reykjavik University, Bucharest University – faculty of Physics and SC OPTOELECTRONICA-2001 SA (OPTOEL, Romanian SME) developed and implemented a project funded by EEA Grants, more specifically, Perovskites for Photovoltaic Efficient Conversion Technology, PERPHECT, project [10], [11] (see Figure 3).

The project team, coordinated by Dr. Ioana Pintilie (senior researcher at NIMP), managed to achieve perovskite solar cells with photovoltaic conversion efficiency of 15.4% representing PCE record values for Romania.

Some of the market available techniques and their specific equipment to be used for deposition of ultra-thin layers in are presented next.

(a) Wire-Bar Coating

Wire-bar coating is a simple deposition method for preparing large areas of organic films at low cost and processes developed on such equipment are amenable to scale-up

It has particular benefits, including excellent control of solidification rate and deposition temperature, compatibility with flexible substrates, capability for a wide range of substrate sizes, from mm to tens of cm, plus a high degree of coating reproducibility. Controlled deposition speed and pressure are important factors in achieving high quality films, which are applied by wire wound bars which meter the ink used for coating, the thickness being controlled by the diameter of the wire, as well as the ink formulation and ambient conditions.

Organic blend thin films consisting of semiconducting poly(3-hexylthiophene) (P3HT) and insulating high-density polyethylene (HDPE) have been fabricated by novel application of a large area wire-bar coating technique in air. Thin films of organic samples were produced by a wirebar coating deposition method, using a K101 K Control Coater from RK PrintCoat Instruments Ltd [12].

A typical bar-coating machine consists of a coating bar sitting above a substrate (flexible or rigid), and usually a moving mechanism that enables the substrate to move against the coating bar. A standard bar-coating process consists in three major steps (see Figure 4).

1. the horizontal transport of the substrate against the coating bar;
2. the wet coating of the polymer film;
3. the film drying

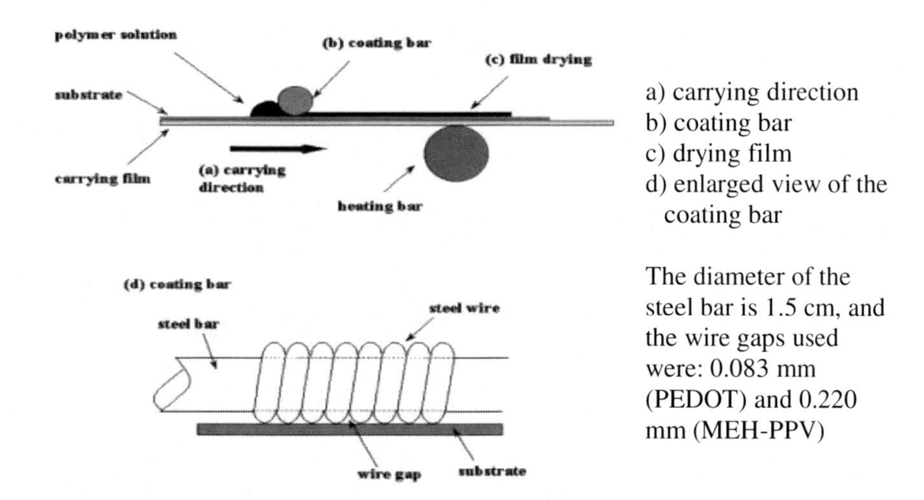

Figure 4. Scheme of the wire-bar coating process [13].

In the study [13] a bar-coating machine was specially designed and constructed to operate inside a standard glove-box. It allows the continuous coating of polymeric films on both rigid and flexible substrates in an inert gas environment. There were used flexible pre-patterned indium tin oxide (ITO)/polyethylene terephthalate (PET) substrate. A sufficient amount of polymer solution (conjugated polymers for light emitting diodes) was placed close to the leading edge of the substrate. The carrying speed was 10 cm/s. The temperature of the heater was 70°C. The gap size and the concentration of the polymer solution were the main factors determining the final thickness of the film.

Wire-bar coating equipment produced by RK PrintCoat Instruments [14] is shown in Figure 5.

(b) Doctor Blade (Frame)

Doctor blade (or tape casting) is one of the widely used techniques for producing thin films on large area surfaces. In the doctor blading process, a well-mixed slurry consisting of a suspension of ceramic particles along with other additives (such as binders, dispersants or plasticizers) is placed on a substrate beyond the doctor blade. When a constant relative movement is established between the blade and the substrate, the slurry spreads on the substrate to form a thin sheet which results in a gel-layer upon drying. The doctor blading can operate at a speed up to several meters per minute and it is suitable to coat substrate with a very wide range of wet film thicknesses ranging from 20 to several hundred microns [16].

Mentioned as one of the technologies for flexible solar cell it is not recommended to produce the organic solar cell. Compared to the spin coating, its solution loss is under 5%. It is very low. The thickness of the coating layer (10 ~ 500 μm) is controlled by the gap between the sharp blade and the substrate. The final thickness is a half of the gap. It depends on the surface energy of the substrate, the surface tension of the solution, the viscosity, and the meniscus of the thin film.

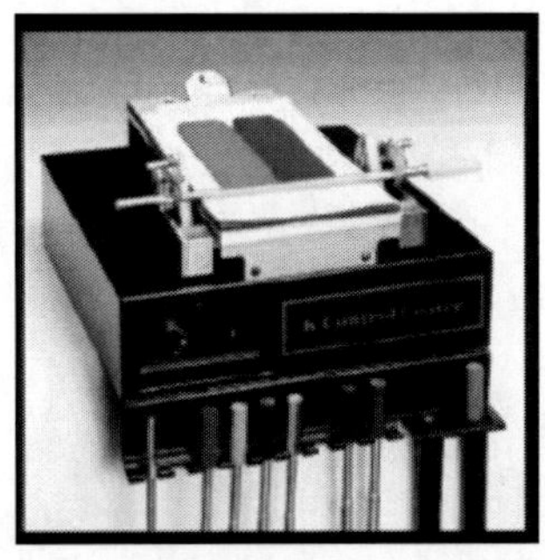

model K 101

Main Features:
- controlled speed and pressure ensure repeatable results
- coating by wire wound bars or gap applicators
- easy to use, easy to clean
- vacuum, magnetic, heated and glass beds available
- two models offering coated areas up to 170 x 250mm or 325 x 250mm
- standard coating speeds infinitely variable between 2 and 15m/min

A meter bar is produced by winding precision drawn stainless steel wire on to a stainless steel rod resulting in a pattern of identically shaped grooves. These grooves then precisely control the wet film thickness. Close wound bars will produce coating thickness from 4 to 120μm.

Higher coating weights up to 500μm can be obtained using spirally wound bars.

STANDARD K101 AND K202 METER BARS

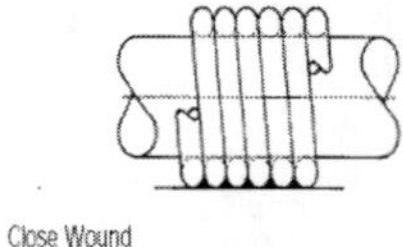
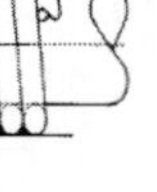
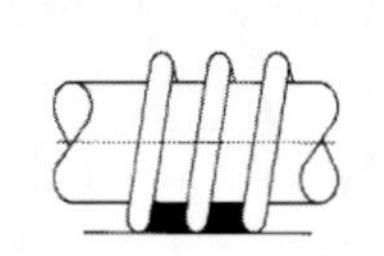

Close Wound

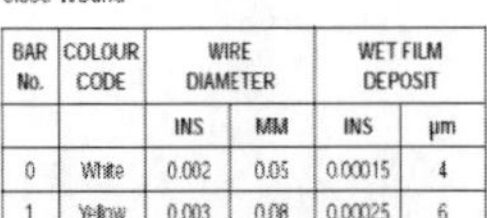

BAR No.	COLOUR CODE	WIRE DIAMETER		WET FILM DEPOSIT	
		INS	MM	INS	μm
0	White	0.002	0.05	0.00015	4
1	Yellow	0.003	0.08	0.00025	6
2	Red	0.006	0.15	0.0005	12

Spirally Wound

BAR No.	WIRE DIAMETER		WET FILM DEPOSIT	
	INS	MM	INS	μm
150	0.010	0.25	0.006	150
200	0.014	0.36	0.008	200
300	0.020	0.51	0.012	300

Figure 5. K Control Coater [15].

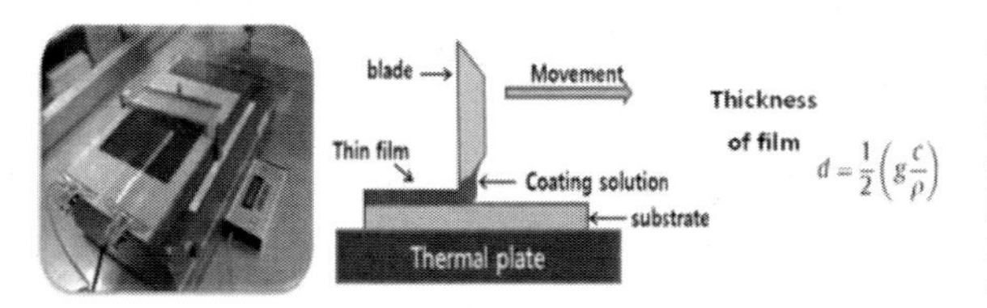

d is the thickness,
g is the gap between the substrate and the blade,
c is the solid content [g/cm3],
ρ is the final density[g/cm3] of the thin film.

Figure 6. Doctor-Blade coating Process [17].

Regarding to the shearing stress, that is generated by the blade movement, the linear velocity (1 ~ 100 mm/s) is not high when the device stress is low. In addition, the loss solution is little so that it is easy to produce thin films. The scheme and equipment of this process is presented in Figure 6 [17].

(c) Screen Printing

The principle of screen printing is shown in Figure 7. A pattern is photographically defined on a stainless steel screen by means of an emulsion layer. A paste of the material to be screen printed is pressed through the screen by means of a squeegee. Important screen printing parameters are: the viscosity of the paste, the mesh number of the screen (# of meshes per inch), the snap-off distance between the screen and the substrate and the pressure and speed of the squeegee. After leveling, the printed wet film is dried (e.g., at 120°C, 60 min).

In [17] it is defined the screen printing as a way inserting paste into the opening of the dense mesh screen made of plastic or metal fiber in order to form asking shape on the substrate. This method forms patterns on the screen with emulsion that the solution is not stained on emulsion. That is, after moving the screen filled with solutions on the surface without emulsion toward the substrate, by pressing the screen with the squeeze, the screen paste is printed on the substrate. At this point, the total paste is not printed. It depends on the squeeze pressure, the squeezing distance, the squeeze moving speed, and the solution viscosity (see Figure 8).

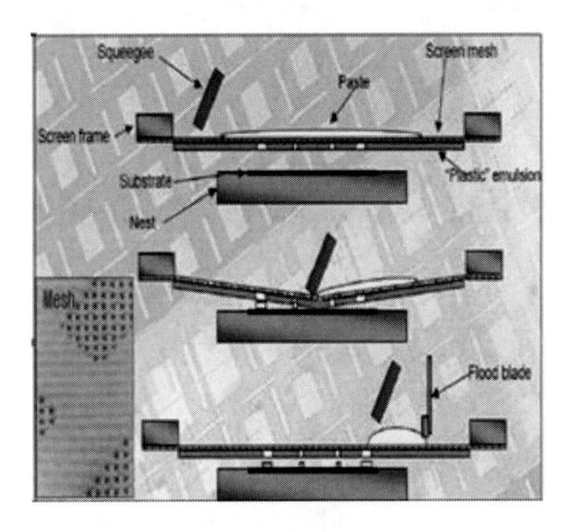

Figure 7. Illustration of the screen printing process [17].

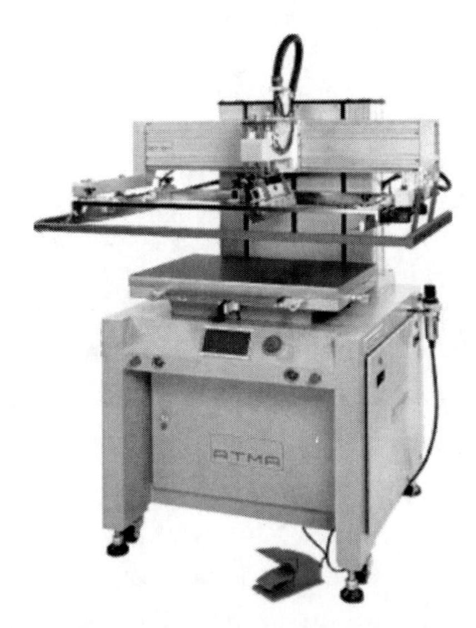

Figure 8. Screen Printer Dyesol [18].

Screen printing equipment, produced by Dyesol company is shown in Figure 8. Some of its characteristics [18] are as follows:

- typically used for the application of an electrical conductor to form a busbar, a catalyst paste to form the counter electrode and a semiconductor paste to form the working electrode;

- flexible nature of this piece of equipment allows users to experiment with the application of other cell components such as electrolytes and sealants;
- controllable squeegee speed and controllable pressure allow for precise and repeatable prints for both small and large production runs. Operation is semi-automatic or manual.

As previously mentioned, there is a high interest in Romania on renewable energy and, specially, on solar energy – as there is a long period with sun "smiling" without clouds.A group of research institutes, universities and SME from Romania, Norway and Iceland joined for a project funded by EEA grants, whose title is "Perovskites for Photovoltaic Efficient Conversion Technology, PERPHECT" [10]. The main objective of the project is to develop perovskite-based photovoltaic devices towards "all perovskite" solar cells with power conversion efficiencies approaching 20% and fabricated with affordable, environmental friendly materials and technologies.

The specific objectives are: 1) to understand the mechanisms behind the high efficiency obtained using a hybrid halide perovskite as visible-light absorber; 2) to increase the PCE by using oxide perovskites with ferroelectric properties (e.g., $BaTiO_3$) as carrier transporter; 3) to develop flexible solar cells by replacing the ITO/FTO transparent electrode with metallic nanowebs. The final goal is to adapt the lab solution-processed deposition to a screen printing technology including the possibility of replacing also the thin counter electrode (usually Ag) with transparent metallic nanowebs. This type of cell, transparent on both sides, enables harvesting both the Sun and indoor light if applied on glass windows.

After selecting the suitable printing technology a demonstrator equipment (prototype), named PERPHECT Printer, was designed and manufactured by the industrial SME partner. It is used for the deposition of ultra-thin successive layer (of perovskite solar cells) with different physical-chemical characteristics, as "proof of concept" on the final test structures.

The Printer, designed and manufactured by the team members of SME project partner and the team from project coordinator is innovative due to the fact that enables three different printing techniques for deposition of ultra-thin layers. In fact it is one equipment, instead of three different equipment - available on the nowadays market [19] and due to its modular structure. It is used for either of three deposition techniques, Wire Bar, Screen Printing, Doctor Blade (see Figure 9).

This innovative Printer ensures the transfer of laboratory technology towards industrial technology, so that stable and efficient cells to be obtained. In fact, it is a relatively cheap technology for obtaining perovskite solar cells based on printing techniques.

This is how, large dimensions (A4 format, 210 x 294, mm x mm) solar cells can be obtained, both on rigid, and flexible substrates.

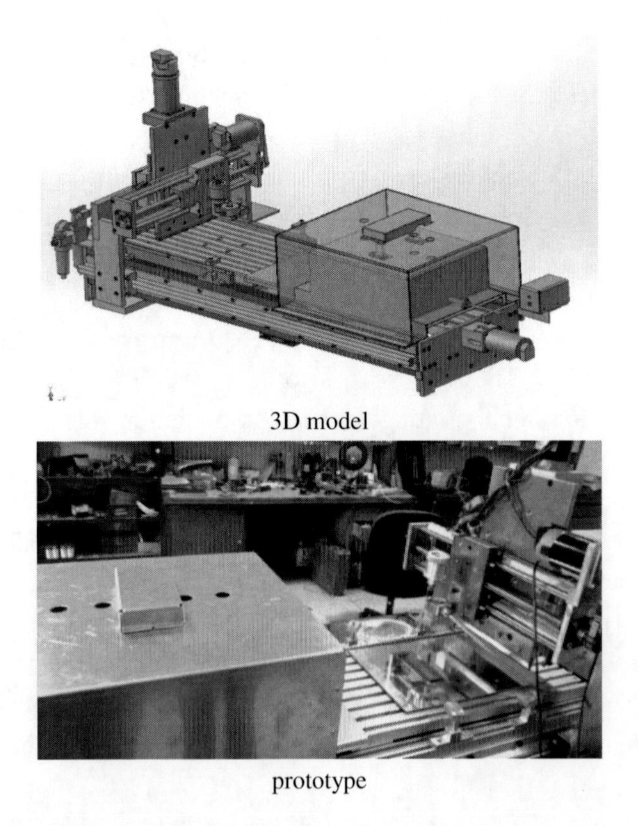

3D model

prototype

Figure 9. Printer "PERPHECT".

3. Electric E-Motion

The number of second-hand cars registered in Romania in the first month of 2018 was 39,261 units [20], more than five times higher than in the similar period of 2017, when only 7,708 units were registered. At national level (Romania), at the end of year 2017, out of the total number of vehicles 5.996 million were cars, more specifically an increase of 9.5% compared to the end of year 2016. According to the Registry (Department of Driving License and Vehicle Registration, DRPCIV), approximately 2.28 million units of the total national fleet were older than 11-15 years, 1,774 million units between 16 and 20 years old, 1,719 million over 20 years old. In addition, by the end of 2017, 3,715,483 vehicles with gasoline engines and 3,501,491 diesel cars were running on Romanian road

In March, 2018, in Romania started the governmental program “Rabla Plus”, that encourages inhabitants to buy hybrid, or electric cars, by awarding each buyer approximately 10,000 euro subventions. As result of this program [21], in the first four months of year 2018, 1,003 electric cars were sold, in comparison with 548 units in the same period of year 2017. Out of the 1,003 cars, 238 were 100% electric cars and 765 were hybrids.

Renewable energy, friendly environment, transportation and, not the least, passion for cars, represent the bases for foundation of a private company, named E-Motion Electric [22]. Its main objective is to promote the concept of electric mobility, being the first Romanian company with activity 100% focused on e-mobility. E-Motion Electric is first of all a manufacturer of power stations for electric vehicles and offers its experts knowledge for the optimum solution of charging infrastructure in Romania. To complement the e-mobility portfolio, E-Motion Electric has become the official importer of A2B electric bicycles. In 2011 people from E-Motion Electric managed to install the first public station in Romania and purchased the first electric car brought to Romania. All products and solutions are Romanian achievements that make everyone proud.

Some of company’s representative products, as well as some of their main characteristics that proof competitiveness (when compared to other similar products available on the market) are presented next.

(a) E-Motion Wall Box and E-Motion Street Box - Technical Specifications (see Figure 10)

Charging points	1 socket – Type 2 1 socket – Schuko Optional with flat cable type 1 or type 2 or spiral cable type 2
Charging performance	up to 22kW 32A 3Phase – 400V
Authorization	Standard: ON/OFF Button Optional: Key-switch
System integration	Modbus RS485
Connectors	Variant with meter: S0 interface
Conformity	According to IEC 61851-1 Mode 3, CE-Conform, Variant with meter (MID-Conform)

(b) E-Motion Fast Charger – Technical Specifications

Charging points	Standard: Dual CCS + CHAdeMO Optional: Additional 22kW or 43kW AC Type 2 charger
Charging performance	up to 50kW 32A 3Phase – 400V
Authorization	RFID MIFARE ISO/IEC14443A/B, ISO/IEC15693, ISO/IEC18000-3, FeliCa, NFC, EMV 2.0
System integration	Standard: OCPP 1.5 3G, GSM and Gigabit Ethernet
Protection	Short circuit protection Over current protection Residual current protection
Conformity	According to IEC 61851-1 Mode 3, CE-Conform, Variant with meter (MID-Conform)

(c) E-Bike [22], [23]

Named for Graeme 'The flying Scotsman' Obree, the radical bicycle innovator, the Obree's brief was to push e-bike boundaries. Since 2008, when A2B designed the first true e-bike for the A2B range, the intention was to create a mode of transportation in its own class, so not just adding a battery on a bicycle, which would seriously hinder the design, stability and look of the product. Six years on, the Obree is one of a new generation of e-bikes, with a much more streamlined look and is also lighter in weight (see Figure 11).

Therefore, the inspiration for refining e-bikes, comes from the desire to incorporate the latest design techniques in order to improve weight, stability and look, but also take into consideration the size and cost requirements of navigating increasingly congested cities and the rising cost of transportation.

Figure 10. E-Motion Street Box and Wall Box.

Figure 11. E-bike, A2B [23].

As several times mentioned before, electric cars are so very environmental friendly so, more and more people decide to buy. Still, in Romania, the charging infrastructure hasn't been developed yet according to drivers needs. This is why, on www.plugshare.com site, one can look for locations of electric vehicles (EV) charging stations, so that to organize the route and avoid lack of chance when electric car charging is needed (see Figure 12).

As mentioned in [24], in Romania there is an evident need for expanding the infrastructure of EV charging stations. Each of these stations has mechanical components where prescribed geometrical precision parameters must be obtained, as result of their machining process, usually milling and/or drilling.

Some research results, meaning regression models to be used for improving cutting tools durability and, finally, the efficiency of machining process, are evidenced by relationship (1):

- for the milling process

$$F_y = -90.269 + 0.248 \cdot v + 22.974 \cdot a_r - 0.054 \cdot v \cdot a_r$$

- for the drilling process (1)

$$F_z = 5.936 + 6.673 \cdot D + 103.75 \cdot f + 0.088 \cdot v_c + 64.375 \cdot D \cdot f - 0.048 \cdot D \cdot v_c$$

where:

- for milling: v is cutting speed (peripheral speed of the cutting tool) [m/min];
  a_r - radial depth (of the cut) [mm];
  F_y - the tangential cutting force component [daN]
- for drilling: D is tool diameter [mm]; f - feed rate [mm/rot];
  v_c - drilling speed [m/min]; F_z - vertical cutting force [N].

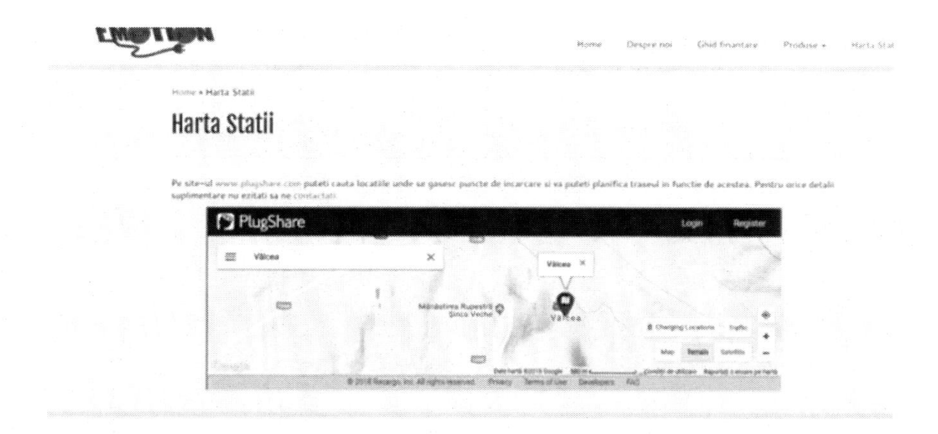

Figure 12. Charging stations location.

4. LGS Buildings

Construction market in Romania, has been revigorating, since 2016, oriented, specially, on environmentally friendly and sustainable constructions.

The metallic constructions, made of Light Gauge Steel (LGS) load bearing systems are getting into the interest of many people, due to their specific benefits, mentioned next [25].

- Steel is a stable material with consistent chemical attributes. Once the steel stud has been formed, it will remain straight with virtually no change to thickness, width or other dimensional properties.
- Steel has a significantly higher strength-to-weight ratio than wood. A steel frame is typically one-third the weight of a wood frame. Consequently, damage through 'inertia' will be significantly reduced since there is less weight to move during an earthquake, and less weight that must stop.
- The building codes used in the design of steel framed walls are based on more rigorous testing procedures put into place after the recent (California) earthquakes of the last decade.

- Steel is non-combustible and does not contribute fuel to the spread of a fire. This can be an important factor should an earthquake's devastation produce fires.

Figure 13. Construction of LGS house (121 sqm).

Some more other advantages are: high recycling for waste of materials used for construction; efficient manufacturing process of the LGS pofiles; whole subassemblies are prodced and labelled within the manufacturing proces and, further, direct transportation to the buiding place; if required, dismantling the construction and relocation, or recovery of its components. Last, but not least, the usable area of construction is larger (when compared to other construction type), for same built-up area, due to the fact that wall thickness is smaller than that of bricks.

In Romania, there is "CASA METALICĂ" company [26], founded in 2005, that offeres high quality LGS based constructions. Its business model is clear - speedy in execution using the latest technology and unbeatable quality at competitive prices. This successful formula now allows to finish construction from scratch in less than 3 months at European standards. Examples of LGS construction are presented in Figure 13.

One branch of this company, TOP AMBIENT SRL, has been funded a project on EU funds, named "Construcţii metalice ecologice şi sustenabile prin tehnologii eficiente de fabricare/Friendly environment and Sustainable Metallic Constructions by Efficient Manufacturing Technologies, TOP MetEco AMBIENT" [27], This project aims is to develop a system of intelligent buildings, by lowering the seismic risk, integrated into the smart city concept of 2020 Romania.

These type of buildings are built on Light Gauge Steel (LGS) load bearing systems. The mechanical caratersitics of LGS profiles' material are improved by induction hardening and scientific research (in this project) is focused on optimization of induction process parameters and increase effiecinecy of LGS profile manufacturing process.

Some preliminary research results, as the project is still in implementation, are evidenced in Figure 14. There are presented characteristic aspects of induction hardening process like: 3D model of one type of LGS profile (420 mm ength); clamping device for LGS profile induction hardening; metaollgraphic structure of LGS profile's materal (S355 steel) and one sample of HV hardeness measurement.

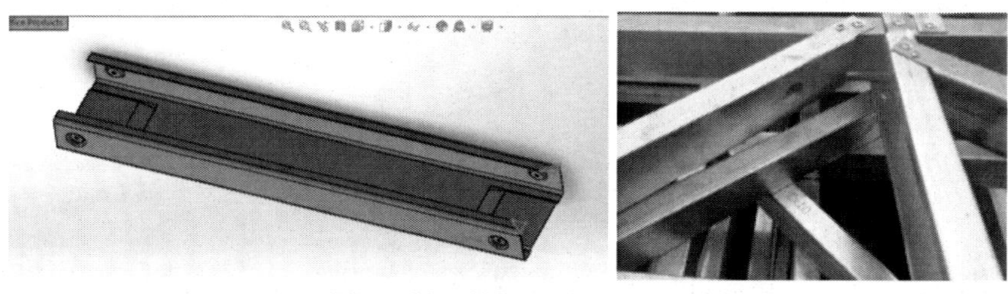

LGS profile (420 mm length type)

horizontal axis for LGS profile vertical axis for LGS profile

clamping device for induction hardening

Figure 14. (Continued).

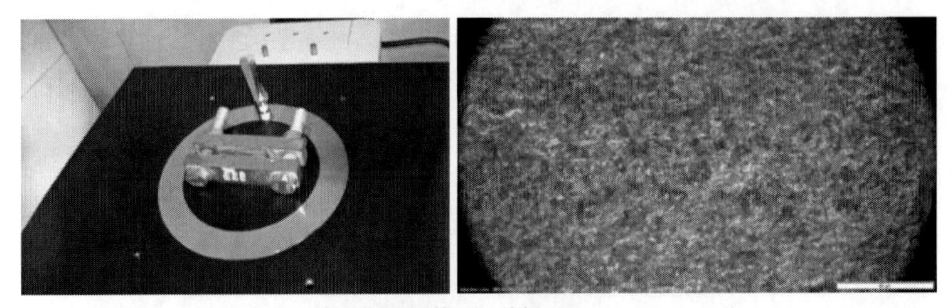

check metallographic structure

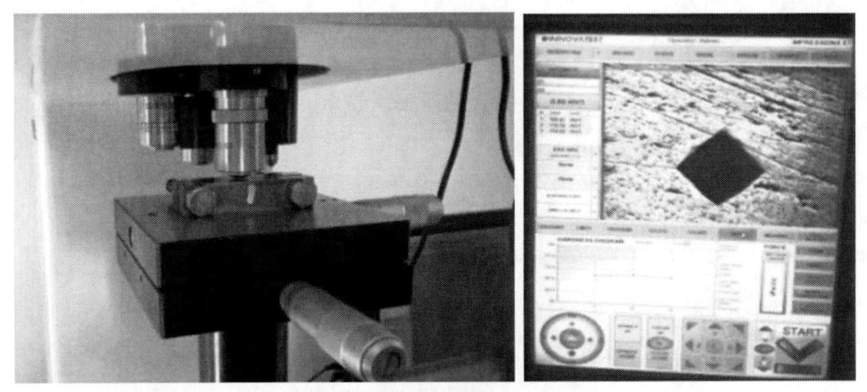

determine HV hardness values

Figure 14. Study on induction hardening of LGS profile.

Figure 15. Failure of LGS profiles in house foundation.

There was the inquiry on what could be done so that to improve mechanical characterisitics of LGS profile material. It was considered to be of benefit this improvement, bcause, many times, the LGS structure, specially the ones in foundations broke out (see Figure 15). In order to solve this issue, there have been considered many options like: changing material type of metallic profiles, annealing the profile, using extra components to improve stiffness in truss. Due to the reduced thickness of LGS profile material and, also, due to machining process type (roll cold plastic deformation) it should be a balance, from the point of view of carbon percentage (%C). More specifically, if the carbon percentage is high (more than 0.4%) then hardening process would be significant but, difficulties and material damages will appear in roll cold plastic deformation. On the contrary, if the carbon content is low (less then 0.2%) then roll deformation would be without problems (no cracks or, failures) but the hardening process would not be significant (no hardness increase).

The only thermal treatment that fits for LGS profile material (carbon content of 0.2 ÷ 0.4%C) is estimated to be induction hardening, with high /medium frequency currents. By this way, the failure resistance of LGS profile material would be increased, so that it is estimated a better behaviour in exploitation and lack of failures.

CONCLUSION

This chapter is aimed to point out some relevant aspects, both scientific and commercial, of the interest in renewable energy, electric motion and eco-construction, in Romania of the 2010s.

The first aspect is that of renewable energy, more specific, of photovoltaic and solar cells. Here there are evidenced: research results on, relatively, affordable technology of producing perovskite solar cells, stable enough and conversion efficiency of 15.4% (PCE record values for Romania); prototype of the printer used for successive deposition of ultra-thin layers (components of perovskite solar cells),with different physical-chemical characteristics.

The second aspect refers to e-motion, more specific electric vehicles and the infrastructure of charging stations. There are evidenced some commercial aspects, products designed, made and sold by Romanian company, E-MOTION ELECTRIC. Also, some scientific research results on optimization of manufacturing process for mechanical components of EV charging stations are presented (regression models of force).

solar energy - used in countryside [28]

Kaufland parking, Bucharest

LGS load bearing system house

real Green – trees and flowers on Bucharest streets

Figure 16. Romania looking forward "Green".

The third aspect is of ecological and sustainable constructions, made of low thickness steel proiles. These Light Gauge Steel (LGS) buildings, made of load bearing systems are the ones to ensure low pollution, high efficiency and incredible earthquake resistance. Some research results on induction hardening process for LGS profiles are also presented.

Finally, the conclusion is that Romania looks towards green – energy, e-motion, eco-buildings and its population is willing to protect enviroment and even better if that results in lower costs for energy, heat, transportation and construction (see Figure 16).

ACKNOWLEDGMENTS

This work is based on research activity carried on while implementation period of projects;

(a) Perovskites for Photovoltaic Efficient Conversion Technology", PERPHECT, no. 8 SEE/30.06.2014
(b) "Construcţii metalice ecologice şi sustenabile prin tehnologii eficiente de fabricare/Friendly environment and Sustainable Metallic Constructions by Efficient Manufacturing Technologies, TOP MetEco AMBIENT", no. 107/09/09.201

REFERENCES

[1] http://www.ziare.com/transelectrica/stiri-transelectrica/jumatate-din-energia-produsa-duminica-in-romania-este-din-surse-regenerabile-1479723 (accessed on May 20, 2018).

[2] https://www.digi24.ro/stiri/sci-tech/auto/programul-rabla-plus-ce-masini-electrice-pot-fi-cumparate-cu-bonusul-de-10-000-de-euro-oferit-de-stat-901928 (accessed on May 20, 2018).

[3] http://www.ziare.com/auto/masini-electrice/vanzarile-de-masini-electrice-si-hibrid-cresc-spectaculos-in-romania-ce-modele-domina-topul-1511680 (accessed on May 20, 2018).

[4] http://www.apia.ro/en/ (accessed on May 20, 2018).

[5] http://www.capital.ro/ce-masini-electrice-puteti-achizitiona-cu-bonus-de-10000-de-euro.html (accessed on May 20, 2018). http://www.loomcraftsprefab.com/copy-of-characteristics-of-steel-bu (accessed on May 20, 2018). http://www.casametalica.ro/constructii-case.html (accessed on May 20, 2018).

[6] http://www.marketwatch.ro/articol/15632/Celule_Solare_cu_Perovskiti_Halogenati__valori_record_pentru_Romania_in_ceea_ce_priveste_eficienta_de_conversie_fotovoltaica_a_energiei_solare__154__la_suta_/ (accessed on May 20, 2018). http://solarcellcentral.com/markets_page.html (accessed on May 21, 2018). http://8see.infim.ro/ (accessed on May 21, 2018). http://8see.infim.ro/docs/leaflet%20A4.pdf (accessed on May 21, 2018).

[7] Craig, E. Murphy; Li, Yang; Santanu, Ray; Liyang, Yu; Steven, Knox; Natalie, Stingelin (2011). "Wire-bar coating of semiconducting polythiophene/insulating polyethylene blend thin films for organic transistors", *Journal of Applied Physics*, http://dx.doi.org/ 10.1063/1.3660779.

[8] Jianyong, Ouyang; Tzung-Fang, Guo; Yang, Yang; Horoyuki, Higuchi; Masahiro, Yoshioka; Tatsuki, Nagatsuka, "High-Performance, Flexible Polymer Light Emitting Diodes Fabricated by a Continuous Polymer Coating Process" (2002). *Advanced Materials Journal*, 14, No. 12, June 18, Wiley-VCH Verlag GmbH, D-69469, Weinheim.

[9] http://www.rkprint.co.uk/ (accessed on November 25, 2014).

[10] "*K Control Coater*", R K Print-Coat Instruments Ltd., www.rkprint.com (accessed on November 10, 2018).

[11] Berni, A; Mennig, M; Schmidt, H. "*Doctor Blade*", http://scidok.sulb.uni-saarland.de/volltexte/2011/3076/pdf/sm200405.pdf (accessed on November 26, 2014).

[12] SNE Research. htm, http://www.sneresearch.com/eng/service/ (accessed on November 26, 2014).

[13] Sean, E. Shaheen; Rachel, Radspinner; Nasser, Peyghambarian; Ghassan, E. Jabbour (2001). "Fabrication of bulk heterojunction plastic solar cells by screen printing", *Applied Physics Letters*, volume 79, no 18.

ILIESCU, M. "Multi-Axes Mechatronic System for Printing Ultrathin Layers of Perovskite Solar Cells - Prototype design and manufacture" (2016), 10th International Conference on Software, Knowledge, Information Management & Applications, *SKIMA* 2016, Chengdu, China (accessed on May 21, 2018). https://www.wall-street.ro/articol/Auto/218036/drpciv-inmatriculari-autoturisme-second-hand-ianuarie-2018.html (accessed on May 22, 2018). https://playtech.ro/2018/romani-masini-electrice/ (accessed on May 22, 2018).

[14] http://e-motionelectric.ro/ev/ (accessed on May 22, 2018).

[15] http://www.wearea2b.com/index.php/ro. http://www.wearea2b.com/index.php/ro/e-bike-collection/ferber (accessed on May 22, 2018).

[16] Iliescu, M; Vlădăreanu, L; Bercan, N; Rogojinaru, A. (2017). "Electric-Motion Infrastructure in Romania – Research on Machining Processes of Mechanical Components of e-Motion Charging Station", pg. 110-124, Communications in Computer and Information Science, Smart Cities, *Green Technologies*, *and Intelligent Transport Systems*, http://www.springer.com/series/7899, ISSN 1865-0929 ISSN 1865-0937 (electronic), ISBN 978-3-319-63711-2, ISBN 978-3-319-63712-9 (eBook), DOI 10.1007/978-3-319-63712-9.

[17] https://www.goldenhomes.co.nz/features/zog-steel-frame-technology (accessed on May 22, 2018).

http://www.casametalica.ro/despre-casa-metalica.html; http://www.casametalica.ro/blog/montaj-structura-metalica-proiect-de-casa-528mp-titan (accessed on May 23, 2018). https://www.fonduri-ue.ro/proiecte/details/1/5857/ (accessed on May 23, 2018).

[18] http://solarcenter.ro/produse/ (accessed on May 23, 2018).

[19] M. ILIESCU, "Multi-Axes Mechatronic System for Printing Ultrathin Layers of Perovskite Solar Cells - Prototype design and manufacture", 10th International Conference on Software, Knowledge, Information Management & Applications, SKIMA 2016, December 15-17, 2016, Chengdu, China (accessed on May 21, 2018)

[20] https://www.wall-street.ro/articol/Auto/218036/drpciv-inmatriculari-autoturisme-second-hand-ianuarie-2018.html (accessed on May 22, 2018)

[21] https://playtech.ro/2018/romani-masini-electrice/ (accessed on May 22, 2018)

[22] http://e-motionelectric.ro/ev/ (accessed on May 22, 2018)

[23] http://www.wearea2b.com/index.php/ro; http://www.wearea2b.com/index.php/ro/e-bike-collection/ferber (accessed on May 22, 2018)

[24] M. Iliescu, L. Vlădăreanu, N. Bercan and A. Rogojinaru, „Electric-Motion Infrastructure in Romania – Research on Machining Processes of Mechanical Components of e-Motion Charging Station", pg.110-124, Communications in Computer and Information Science, Smart Cities, Green Technologies, and Intelligent Transport Systems, http://www.springer.com/series/7899, ISSN 1865-0929 ISSN 1865-0937 (electronic), ISBN 978-3-319-63711-2, ISBN 978-3-319-63712-9 (eBook), DOI 10.1007/978-3-319-63712-9

[25] https://www.goldenhomes.co.nz/features/zog-steel-frame-technology (accessed on May 22, 2018)

[26] http://www.casametalica.ro/despre-casa-metalica.html; http://www.casametalica.ro/blog/montaj-structura-metalica-proiect-de-casa-528mp-titan (accessed on May 23, 2018)

[27] https://www.fonduri-ue.ro/proiecte/details/1/5857/ (accessed on May 23, 2018)

[28] http://solarcenter.ro/produse/ (accessed on May 23, 2018)

In: Romania
Editor: Sophie Clarke
ISBN: 978-1-53614-590-8
© 2018 Nova Science Publishers, Inc.

Chapter 3

THE PARLIAMENTARY ELECTIONS OF 1937 AND 44 DAYS OF THE O. GOGA GOVERNMENT: THE SEARCH FOR A POLITICAL CHOICE IN THE LATE 1930S

Ihor Piddubnyi*
Department of Mordern and Contemporary History,
Yurii Fedkovich National University, Chernivtsi, Ukraina

ABSTRACT

The political crisis of December 1937 in Romania caused the formation of the government of O. Goga, the chairman of the National Christian Party. The personal decision of the King Carol II gave hope for a long reign, in connection with which intensive preparations for the new parliamentary elections were held. The activities of the government were also interrupted by the King's decision to establish authoritatively on February 11 1938.

* Corresponding Author Email: zymnyy@ukr.net.

Keywords: Octavian Goga, National Christian Party, National Liberal Party, Armand Călinescu

INTRODUCTION

The political life of the Kingdom of Romania between the wars was characterized by two periods when practically the same political leaders were in power, albeit in different political conditions. Thus, the period from December 1918 to December 1937 could be characterized as the period of parliamentary democracy, while the period from February 1938 to September 1940 – as the authoritarian period. However, from December 1937 to February 11, 1938, the regime in the country was represented by the members of the National Christian anti-Semitic party, whose activities set up the conditions for transition to the authoritarian form of government. The lack of king's trust in this political force pushed him to include in the government the people who had to defend his political interests and then he made one of the ministers (A. Călinescu) a leading figure of the regime during the next period. The issue of transition from the democratic model to the authoritarian government in the country has already been discussed in the works of a number of the Romanian (F. Nedelcu, A. Sava, G. Pop, I. Scurtu) and English-speaking (K. Hitchins, J. Rottschild) historians. This study is an attempt to highlight certain aspects of O. Goga's long-term stay in power.

New Romania established in late 1918, also known as *Greater Romania,* united territories of four states, underwent a rather complicated path during the interwar period. No less difficult was the political life in the country, which by the end of the 1930s led to the formation of more than fifty political parties and organizations trying to take a certain place in the political life of the country. However, only a small number of parties remained among those that were able to get into the parliament. The parliamentary elections in December 1937 demonstrated a certain gap with the existing tradition giving them the opportunity to gain significantly more votes for right-wing radical organizations and preventing the government from acting in power. From that very moment, changes began in the political system of the country.

The country with the oligarchic system of power underwent significant changes in the political system in the 1930s. The fall of trust in the "historical parties," like the National Liberal Party and National Peasants' Party, increased support of the right-wing radical forces, and the strengthening of nationalist sentiments among the intelligentsia illustrated the political life in the country. It was also not surprising that during the parliamentary election of December 1937 none of the "historical parties" won the necessary 40% of votes. The impossibility for the NLP to remain in power alone or in a coalition with the other party was the reason for Gh. Tătărescu's resignation.

However, the National Liberal Party (NLP) itself did not intend to abandon power and initiated measures to strengthen the party organization. However, in the current situation, the king had to resolve the issue of the successor not allowing the legionnaires to enter the open political crisis and power. The desire to weaken the Legionary movement encouraged the king to choose a party that would become a successor and it was the National Christian Party (NCP) with 9.8% of votes at the elections.

It is possible that after the parliamentary elections they intended to set up the Gheorghe Tătărescu – Octavian Goga coalition government but that step could not have succeeded and on December 27 the decision on the government demise was made. On the part of the king, there were no consultations on the creation of a new government and the decision was made to create the government consisting of the NCP and National Peasants Party members. The reason for such decision was just the third place in the election of the "All for the Country" party, which was considered the highest achievement of Corneliu Z. Codreanu in his entire political career in Romania. Until December 28, 1937, the government of Gheorghe Tătărescu remained in power. In fact, during that period, decisions were taken on the further actions of the king. On December 23, Ernest Urderianu informed Armand Călinescu about the decision of the king to control the events and to immediately establish the government headed by Octavian Goga. On December 24, 1937 night, Octavian Goga and Armand Călinescu held a meeting on the government program, which O. Goga discussed with the king during his afternoon audience on December 23. Preparations for the change of government led to the king's coming to Bucharest from Sinai on December 26, 1937, which was made secretly without telling the members of the government and the government was dissolved on December 28. The attitude towards a new candidacy for the head of the government was relevant in the Western states. Even after the removal of the Octavian Goga government, *Daily Herald* wrote on February 12, 1938, that the king hoped to strike Corneliu Z. Codreanu by the appointment of "Semi-Fascist Octavian Goga," which might be true in the case when it was believed that through the activities of the Octavian Goga government the ground for establishing the regime of king's personal power was prepared. In that case, the choice of Armand Călinescu, the representative of the center forces in the NPP, was also not random if we consider his attitude toward Iuliu Maniu and the issues of constitutional reform in the country, the problems of relations with the guardists. A. Călinescu himself was regarded by the government as a person who served as a kind of observer in the government, and at the same time, a counterweight to I. Maniu for the party. There were Istrate Micescu, General Gabriel Marinescu, General Bengliu, General Paul Teodorescu to support A. Călinescu in the government activities, the O. Goga's government formation caused a warning and panic among the Jewish population of the country. One of the first signs of change was the government's ban on the *Lupta* newspaper published by the Fagure-Honigman brother[1].

On December 29, 1937 night, the new Council took an oath. O. Goga took office as a Council chairman, while Alexandru C. Cuza was appointed the state minister. A. Călinescu – the Minister of the Interior, I. Micescu was appointed the Minister of Foreign Affairs, V. Potîrke – the Minister of Public Works and Communications, V. Rădulescu-Mehedinţi – the

[1]Nedelcu, F. (1973). *Viaţa politică din România în preajma instaurării dictaturii regale*. Cluj: Dacia, p.167-169, 173-174; Arhivele Naţionale ale României (Bucureşti), fond *Direcţia Generală a Poliţiei, 2350, dosar Nr. 17/1937*, fila 96. [*Political life in Romania near the establishment of royal dictatorship*. Cluj: Dacia, p.167-169, 173-174; National Archives of Romania (Bucharest), fund *Directorate General of Police, 2350, file Nr. 17/1937*, fil].

Minister of Justice, E. Savu – Minister of Finance, I. Petrovici – the Minister of National Education, I. Lupaş – the Minister of Cults and Arts, I. Antonescu was appointed the Minister of Defence, R. Irimescu – the Minister of Air and Maritime Affairs, C. Banu – the Minister of Health, G. A. Cuza – the Minister of Labor, S. Giţescu – the Minister of Cooperation. Former NPP member D. Simian was appointed Undersecretary of the Ministry of Internal Affairs. Among the ministers of the new government, there were at least four representatives of the NPP, and A. Călinescu was distinguished by his traits among them. The people who were supposed to have been those who actually belonged to the "people of the king" were among new members of the Council. The king's address to the new government contained a message of confidence which said that they were trusted by the country at a difficult time and something that could not have been done without a thorough consideration by the king. In fact, the appointment of the government proved to be demonstration for political parties that no political force would succeed in the country without the royal agreement. The Council itself was considered almost authoritarian, it was composed of persons, who the king could manage at his own discretion. The arrival of the government also demonstrated the possibility of anarchy in the country, although the king's actions were directed both against the legionnaires and against I. Maniu. O. Goga himself really believed that there wouldn't be any peace in the country due to the C.Z. Codreanu actions[2]. Inclusion of the NPP representatives in the government was also the king's decision aimed at deepening the crisis in the party and preventing the strengthening of the NCP's position in the country. The appointment of A. Călinescu was the reason for his group's departure from the party and reformatting its basis. This was accompanied

[2]Scurtu, I. (1983). *Din viaţa politică a României (1926-1947): Studiu critic privind istoria Partidului Naţional-Ţărănesc.* Bucureşti: Editura ştiinţifică şi enciclopedică, p. 388-390; Sonea, E.,& Sonea, G. (1978).*Viaţa economică şi politică a României. 1933-1938.* Bucureşti: Editura ştiinţifică şi enciclopedică, p. 277-281. [*From the Political Life of Romania (1926-1947): Critical Study on the History of the National Peasant Party.* Bucharest: Scientific and Encyclopedic Publishing House, pp. 388-390; Sonea, E., & Sonea, G. (1978). *Economic and Political Economy of Romania. 1933-1938.* Bucharest: The Scientific and Encyclopaedic Publishing House, pp. 277-281].

by a situation in which the left-wing members could join Gh. Iunian, and supporters of I. Maniu – the Guardists or the Constitutional Bloc.

On December 29, 1937, the government meeting was held in the presence of all ministers. The regulations of Council activities were defined, and the head of government presented the main provisions of his radio speech on occasion of the New Year. The first administrative measures that intended to be put into action immediately for the purpose of the government program implementation were identified. The essence of administrative measures, which the government began to implement, was the immediate replacement of public councils throughout the country. At the same time, it was decided to transfer censorship of the press from the Ministry of Internal Affairs directly to the Council of Ministers and to state undersecretary A. Godoş[3].

The appointment of General I. Antonescu, against which the king objected, was one of the problems. Unlike the king, A. Călinescu supported the general. C.Z. Codreanu expressed his wish that the Minister of National Defense guaranteed security of the Legionnaires' movement. I. Antonescu promised to keep the army from any actions against the guardists. Actually, the collaboration of the king and the general had lasted only until the establishment of dictatorship. The internal party disagreement became one more issue for the government. Thus, the appointment of A.C. Cuza took advantage of the latter as he was going to implement the program of the party through government activities. But there were more representatives of the gogists in the government – I. Lupaş, E. Savu, I. Dragomir, S. Bornemis, A. Godoş, A. Baciu, L. Scridon, L. Blaga. Among them, only I. Lupaş and S. Dragomir were well-known to the general public. Minister of Labor Gh. A. Cuza was the representative

[3](1938). Consiliul de miniştri de Miercuriseara.*Universul, 1 Ianuarie, Nr. 1*, p. 13;(1938). Cenzura presei va trece la Preşedinţia Consiliului. *Universul, 1 Ianuarie, Nr. 1*, p. 13. [Council of Ministers of Miercuriseara.Universitatea, 1 ianuarie, Nr. 1, p. 13 (1938). The censorship of the press will go to the presidency of the Council. The Universe, January 1, Nr. 1, p. 13].

of the Cuza wing of the party. Such a representation in the government could create a split in the party[4].

Meanwhile, the Romanian press published foreign press reviews on the attitude to the new government. Thus, the Polish papers contained articles where they expressed pleasure at coming the centrist and right coalition government to power. *Gazeta Polska* noted profound changes in the government policy, and A.C. Cuza, O. Goga, as well as Foreign Minister I. Micescu provided nationalist character to the government. The country's future was seen in the development of nation, the strengthening of power, the strengthening of the army, and the strengthening of integration processes. The *Maly Dziennik* newspaper believed that the solution of the crisis strengthened monarchical principles of power, and the new government gave an opportunity to focus on the national idea. The German press presented reports about the new government in Romania and they were combined with the publication of O. Goga's biography, as it was associated with a new relationship between the two countries. Opinions about the possibility of depriving Romanian Jews of the social life of the country were also expressed. The Hungarian press abstained from comments, noting the nationalist nature of the government. It was true that O. Goga was called the most acceptable figure in the Danube Confederation. The English press paid attention to the government crisis and its rapid resolution. The Italian press met the news on the nationalist government formation with enthusiasm paying tribute to O. Goga and I. Micescu. The new government was also praised in the Yugoslav press. The French press drew attention to statements by the chairman of the Council of Ministers on the observance of constitutional freedoms. *Le Temps* noted that the government was fully in the constitutional field. The appearance of I. Antonescu in the government was regarded as a friendly step to France. *Excelsior* noted the intentions of the king to maintain the traditional policies of the country[5].

---

[4]Nedelcu, F. (1973). *Viaţa politică din România în preajma instaurării dictaturii regale*. [*Political life in Romania near the establishment of royal dictatorship*]. Cluj: Dacia, p. 176-178.

[5](1938). Presa străină salută cu satisfacţie noul guvern Goga. *Universul, 1 Ianuarie, Nr. 1*, p. 8; (1938). Presa străină despre noul guvern Român. *Universul, 2 Ianuarie, Nr. 2*, p.8. [The

After the formation, the Government's program was promoted and implemented. This activity was regarded as directed against the rights of citizens and democratic freedoms. Actually, the effect of the siege regime was extended, and censorship was transferred to the management by the military authorities under the chairmanship of the Council of Ministers chairman. On December 29, a list of newspapers threatening the "moral health of the country" (*Adevărul, Dimineața* and *Lupta*) was drawn up and traveling by train was restricted to 150 journalists of Jewish origin. The decree-law of January 22, 1938, revoked the consideration of granting citizenship to those who entered the country illegally. Permissions issued to the Jews for selling alcoholic beverages were withdrawn. Some steps to foreign-born personnel displacement were made. Also, the government issued a telegraph order to substitute the district prefects by trusted NCP people. At the same time, the chambers of labor were dissolved and unions were about to be replaced by the guilds after their dissolution[6].

The government activities in the foreign policy were based on its own program, which supported the Rome-Berlin axis and the actual normalization of relations with countries of nationalist orientation. Particularly, the government sought to deepen Italian-Romanian relations. In an interview to the Polish *Poledni List*, O. Goga spoke about a friendly pact with Italy and expansion of relations with Germany. Some intentions of the head of government, like the breakup of relations with France, were banned by the king. In relations with the USSR, the government took the position of reluctance to conclude a pact to maintaining good neighborly relations. Despite declarations on extended relations with Germany and Italy, Romania maintained relations with its old allies, which was in fact acceptable to the Romanian public and, in particular, responded to the

---

foreign press welcomes the new Goga government with satisfaction. *The Universe, January 1, Nr. 1*, p. 8; (1938). Foreign press about the new Romanian government. *The Universe, January 2, 2*, p.8.].

[6](1938). Un început de românizare a presei. *Universul, 1 Ianuarie, Nr. 1*, p. 13(1938). Retragerea licențelor de băuturi spirtoase date evreilor. *Universul, 1 Ianuarie, Nr. 1*, p. 17; Nedelcu, F. (1973). *Viața politică din România în preajma instaurării dictaturii regale*. Cluj: Dacia, p. 179. [A beginning of Romanianization of the press. *The Universe, January 1, Nr. 1*, p. 13 (1938). Withdrawal of licenses for spirits given to Jews. *The Universe, January 1*, Nr. 1, p. 17; Nedelcu, F. (1973). *Political life in Romania near the establishment of royal dictatorship*. Cluj: Dacia, p. 179].

desire of the king and camarilla. The representatives of the government and the party faced reluctance of employees in their work to comply with government orders. The reason for this was the fact that the majority of employees represented NLP and NPP. In addition, the representatives of the NPP center headed by A. Călinescu in the government could pursue a policy close to the positions of national-peasants. But still on December 31, 1937, O. Goga in an audience with F. Fábricius assured the latter that Romania would lead to a friendly agreement with Germany and develop relations with Reich. On January 16, 1938, O. Goga sent instructions to the Ambassador of Romania to Berlin to inform Minister Neurat about the nature of the new Romanian government, which would normalize relations with Germany.

That move of the Romanian government towards Germany raised concerns in Francc and thc United Kingdom. In late December 1937, the counsellor of the French embassy appealed to the king expressing the idea of reluctance to appoint Goga's government, which would undermine confidence in the relations between the two countries. As a result of the Romanian government actions the suspension of the execution of orders by France and Great Britain for the Czechoslovak Republic armament was stopped. The anti-Semitic actions of the government forced the French and British governments to ask O. Goga's government to respect the rights of national minorities. The US interpreted the new government as the victory of the German policy in Central Europe.

The formation of the government caused a certain opposition abroad. At least in a private letter to the king the unknown person (A. Boche) from Paris reported on a conspiracy against the government, caused by persuasion in cooperation with Germany and Italy. Such activities organized through the Ministry of Foreign Affairs led to restrictions on cooperation with French enterprises, which received a loan of 30 million francs and growing pressures in the press. Not surprising was the publication in the Parisian *Marianne*, which was directed against O. Goga, because it called him a Hungarian by birth and noted his cooperation in newspapers and magazines funded by Jews. Commenting on that publication, the *Universul* newspaper noted the deployment of a campaign against Romania[7].

It was disadvantageous to change the policy of Romania to Czechoslovakia, which depended on Romania's position on the issue of confronting Hungarian and German aggression. However, the government's activities in the foreign policy sphere led by the Ministry of Foreign Affairs (I. Micescu), were accepted as being directed by the king. In particular, during the visit of I. Micescu to Prague in January 1938, he assured that Romania was still in the format of the Little Entente. Similar statements in allegiance to the allied relations were also made in Belgrade[8]. However, the most pressing issue was the internal organization of O. Goga's administration. Thus, his interview with K. Kust published in the *Poledny List* newspaper contained assurances of commitment, as well as expressed friendship with Italy and the desire to maintain them with Italy and Germany. *The Daily Telegraph*'s interview with O. Goga contained the rejection of any possibility of establishing a regime similar to fascism and assured of the government's compliance with the constitutional regime. He was also convinced of victory in parliamentary elections, as he believed that Romanian nationalists had numerous supporters. He also argued that the authorities would adhere to the provisions of the treatise on national minorities, but will conduct activities against the invasion of Jews after the war. The number of Jews was within 500 thousand people. Regarding

---

[7]Arhivele Naţionale ale României (Bucureşti), fond *Casa Regală, 727, dosar Nr. 4/1938,* fila 1; (1938). "Marianne" despre Transilvania şi d. Goga... *Universul, 21 Ianuarie, Nr. 20*, p. 5. [National Archives of Romania (Bucharest), *Royal House Fund, 727, file Nr. 4/1938*, file 1; (1938). "Marianne" about Transylvania and Mr. Goga ... *The Universe, 21 January, Nr. 20*, p. 5].

[8]Sonea, E.,& Sonea, G. (1978).*Viaţa economică şi politică a României. 1933-1938.* Bucureşti: Editura ştiinţifică şi enciclopedică, p. 281-284; Pop, Gh.T. (1978). *Caracterul antinaţional şi antipopular al activităţii Partidului Naţional Creştin.* Cluj-Napoca: Dacia, p. 178, 182-187, 190-191, 197-214. [*Economic and Political Economy of Romania. 1933-1938.* Bucharest: Scientific and Encyclopaedic Publishing House, pp. 281-284; Pop, Gh.T. (1978). *The anti-national and antipopular character of the activity of the National Christian Party.* Cluj-Napoca: Dacia, p. 178, 182-187, 190-191, 197-214].

foreign policy, he stressed on the Romanian desire to maintain friendly relations with all countries, including the USSR[9].

Political parties formed an opinion on the government activities. Thus, the communists distrusted the government that was regarded as the eve of the dictatorship in the country. In NLP (D. Brătianu) the NCP was considered a threat to the country due to the creation of anarchy in the country by demagogic agitation. However, the party was not going to oppose the king-appointed government, but they intended to act as advocates of the rule of law and constitutional norms. D. Brătianu believed in the party's coming to power and for this reason he arranged the reorganization of the district organizations of the party. A commission consisting of Gh. Tătărescu, M. Cancicov, I. Inculeţ, C. Brătianu was created. The task of the commission was to develop a circular and instructions on the unity of the actions of party organizations. At the same time, attempts were made to unite the two parts of the liberal party. The NLP (Gh. Brătianu) at the meeting on January 4, 1938, established measures that had to be taken against the government of the NCP. That is why Gh. Brătianu demanded the full power to solve the problem of the party unity. Otherwise, the Georgists were about to create an opposition bloc in an alliance with I. Maniu and C.Z. Codreanu, who had to make a single list in the elections. The king expected the government would act in the direction of nationalism. Positively, the NCP government coming to power was taken in Berlin and regarded it as a step towards the improvement of German-Romanian relations. In the USSR, the appointment of that government was perceived negatively, whereas in Italy the government was perceived as a representative of a new national force, which Italy sincerely welcomed. In the countries where Romania had friendly relations, the new government was accepted negatively[10].

---

[9](1938) Alte două interviewuri ale d-lui prim-ministru Oct. Goga. *Universul, 20 Ianuarie, Nr. 19*, p. 13. [Two other interviews with Prime Minister Oct. Goga. *The Universe, January 20, Nr. 19*, p. 13].

[10]Sonea, E., & Sonea, G. (1978).*Viața economică și politică a României. 1933-1938.* București: Editura ştiinţifică şi enciclopedică, p. 284-285, 286-288; (1937). [*Romania's economic and political life. 1933-1938.* Bucharest: Scientific and Encyclopedic Publishing House, pp. 284-285, 286-288; (1937)]. Правительство Татареску-Ґоґи. *Час, 29 грудня, Ч. 2631*; (1937). Нове правительство Ґоґа-Куза.Час, 30 грудня, Ч. 2632. [Government of

Taking into account this circumstance, Carol II in his speech spoke about the traditions, rights of minorities, which in general could reduce the fuss of the cusists in implementing the party's program[11]. Following him, on January 2, 1938, O. Goga had a keynote speech on the radio, in which he outlined the nationalistic provisions of the program of the party and government promising to resolve the national issue by pushing the national minorities, primarily Jews, from the economic life of the country. The slogan proposed by the chairman of the Council of Ministers corresponded in his vision of the spiritual revival of Rominism and the support of the monarchy. He also mentioned the first steps of the government to resolve the presented program. As a result, a wave of launching actions against the representatives of national minorities swept through the country. In addition to anti-Semitic speeches, in early January 1938, the government issued a decree on the verification of the nationality for national minorities. On January 1, 1938, the government issued instructions to entrepreneurs on making lists of workers and employees of non-Romanian origin. But, the situation that developed in the country was regarded as a dangerous game of the king both for the country and for himself[12].

The supporters of the nationalist movement favored the appointment of the government positively, as nationalist sentiments began to prevail in the public opinion. A number of nationalist organizations began to seek ground for joint actions on the orders that the government had to take. The centrists from the NPP who accepted the proposal to join the government were called patriots. Ordinary citizens expected the government to take appropriate steps, including jobs. The military, both active and those who

---

Tatarese-Gogh. *Hour, December 29, Ch. 2631*; (1937). New Gogh-Cusa Government. Chas, December 30, Ch. 2632].

[11]Iorga, N. (1939). *Memorii, Vol. VII: Sinuciderea partidelor (1932-1938)*. [*Memories, Vol. VII: Suicide of the Parties (1932-1938)*]. București, p. 449.

[12](1938). Cuvântarea-program rostită la radio de d. Octavian Goga, preşedinte consiliul de miniştri. *Universul, 3 Ianuarie, Nr. 3*, p. 3; Языкова, А.А.(1963). *Румыния накануне Второй мировой войны: 1934-1939 гг.* Москва: изд-во АН СССР, с. 207-208; Nedelcu, F. (1973). *Viaţa politică din România în preajma instaurării dictaturii regale*. Cluj: Dacia, p. 184. [The radio program spoken by radio by Octavian Goga, chairman of the council of ministers. *The Universe, 3 January, Nr. 3*, p. 3; Язькова, А.А. (1963). *Romania on the eve of World War II: 1934-1939г.* Moscow: published in the USSR, c. 207-208; Nedelcu, F. (1973). *Political life in Romania near the establishment of royal dictatorship*. Cluj: Dacia, p. 184].

were in reserve, were completely satisfied with the changes. The Jews, who saw in the government's actions the possibility of the citizenship revision and distribution of property, expressed their concerns about the NCP coming to power. Similar sentiments prevailed in Moldova, Bukovyna and Bessarabia, while the leaders of a number of organizations left the country[13].

Among government measures a significant place was occupied by the dissolution of communal and district councils, replacement of prefects and mayors. Almost immediately after coming to power, the government launched a program of replacing mayors and commissions in communities and counties. Since December 29, 1937, such changes occurred in the counties of Bacău, Iaşi, Tîrnava Mare, Severin, on December 30 – the counties of Tutova, Lăpuşna, Hunedoara, Deva. Subsequently, the Ministry of Internal Affairs held preparations for the public and district councils' dissolution. This list was continued by the counties of Maramureş, Constanţa, Tulcea, Rădăuţi, Izmail, Olt, Selaj, Vaslui, CetateaAlbă, Dîmboviţa, Prahova, Rîmnicu Serat, Făgăraş, Romanaţi. On December 31, 1937, a new commission in the municipality of Timişoara headed by G. Andrášiu began its work. Also, in late January 1938, they replaced the prefects in the counties of Putna, Gorj, Buzău, Prahova[14]. In fact, the

[13]Arhivele Naţionale ale României (Bucureşti), fond *Direcţia Generală a Poliţiei, 2350, dosar Nr. 17/1937,* file 94-97, 98,100, 103. [National Archives of Romania (Bucharest), fund *Directorate General of Police, 2350, file Nr. 17/1937*, file 94-97, 98,100, 103].

[14](1938). Instalări de noui prefecţi. *Universul, 1 Ianuarie, Nr. 1*, p.15; (1938). Dizolvarea consiliilor comunale şi judeţene. *Universul, 1 Ianuarie, Nr. 1*, p. 17; (1938). Noui prefecţi de judeţe. *Universul, 2 Ianuarie, Nr. 2*, p. 5;(1938). Instalarea nouei comisii interimare a municipiului Timişoara. *Universul, 2 Ianuarie, Nr. 2*, p. 11; (1938). Noul prefect al jud. Hunedoara. *Universul, 3 Ianuarie, Nr.3*, p.2; (1938). Instalarea noului prefect. *Universul, 3 Ianuarie, Nr.3*, p.2; (1938). La Târnava Mare. *Universul, 3 Ianuarie, Nr.3*, p.2;(1938). La Lugoj. *Universul, 3 Ianuarie, Nr.3*, p.2;(1938). Instalarea prefectului de Constanţa. *Universul, 3 Ianuarie, Nr.3*, p.2; (1938). Schimbări de prefecţi. *Universul, 25 Ianuarie, Nr. 24*, p. 5. [Installations of new prefects. *The Universe, January 1, Nr. 1*, p.15; (1938). Dissolution of communal and county councils. *The Universe, January 1, Nr. 1*, p. 17; (1938). The new prefects of counties. *The Universe, January 2, 2*, p. 5 (1938). Installing the new Interim Commission of Timisoara. *The Universe, January 2, 2*, p. 11; (1938). The new prefect of Hunedoara County. *The Universe, January 3, No. 3*, p.2; (1938). Installing the new prefect. *The Universe, January 3, No. 3*, p.2; (1938). La Târnava Mare. *The Universe, January 3, No. 3*, p. 2 (1938). La Lugoj. *The Universe, January 3, No. 3*, p. 2 (1938). Setting up the prefect of Constanta. *The Universe, January 3, No. 3*, p.2; (1938). Changes of prefects. *The Universe, January 25, Nr. 24*, p. 5].

replacement of prefects and community and district councils was a common event for the Romanian political life since it demonstrated the readiness of the government to hold parliamentary elections and receive local support.

Since the government did not have a parliamentary base a decision to dissolve the parliament and set new parliamentary elections for March 2 and 4-6, 1938, was taken on January 18, 1938. The representatives of the "All for the country" Party also took an active part in the election campaign. In the conditions of situation possible changes on January 17, 1938, the NLP under the leadership of Constantin I.C. Brătianu and the NLP under Gheorghe I. Brătianu united. Explaining these actions, C.I.C. Brătianu declared that it had been done to increase the role of the party as a necessary factor of the parliamentary regime. At the same time, the NLP and NPP took a clear anti-legionary position.

Meanwhile, the government took measures to strengthen its position and ensure continued stay in power. The first event was the replacement of public and district councils and creation of inter-council commissions. Until January 20, 1938, the changes in public councils took place in Dorohoi, Mangalia, Abruda, Broşteni, Bicaz, Bradeţ and other communities, as well as inter-council commissions in the counties of Satu Mare, Rădăuţi, Teleorman, Caraş were created[15].

The removal of foreigners from the economic and political life of the country was a real problem. Mostly it was related to Jews. The removal of the companies established after January 1, 1930, from the country's economy could be considered among such measures an economic attempt can be considered. In that case, the exception were the firms that worked in favor of the country[16].

The army also did not stay out of the government attention as I. Antonescu in his interview for *Giornale d'Italia* insisted on the stability of

[15](1938). Noui comisii interimare comunale judeţene.*Universul, 21 Ianuarie, Nr. 20*, p. 9. [The new interim county commissions. *The University, January 21, Nr. 20*, p. 9].

[16](1938). Comercianţi străini cari au firme înscrise după 1930 nu vor putea rămâne în ţară. *Universul, 21 Ianuarie, Nr. 20*, p.1. [Foreign traders who have companies registered after 1930 will not be able to stay in the country. *The Universe, January 21, 20*, p.1].

the Romanian army and its constant tension due to its common border with the Soviet Union[17].

After ongoing remarks in the press, the government eventually achieved the desired dissolution of the parliament in January 1938, which was made for the first time in the history of the country because it was dissolved without convening. The king made a decree-law announcing the dissolution of the parliament and declaring the elections to the House of Deputies on March 2 and the Senate on March 4, 5, 6, with the next convocation of the Parliament on March 10, 1938. The submission of voter rolls for participation in the elections was a new feature of the scheduled elections, which in fact was the invention of the government. Thus, the old graphic electoral marks were canceled and new ones were set in the form of a system of dots where the ordinary number was marked with an appropriate number of dots. At the same time, the government announced its participation in the elections as the National-Christian and Peasant Union. The representatives of the government were able to register that union for participation in the elections with assistance of J. Bojan, the Secretary General of the Ministry of Finance and due to the order of the head of government. They were followed by the registration of national liberals with R. Franasovich, while the third number was received by the representatives of the Romanian Front, followed by the "All for the Country" (Gh. Clime) Party, and then – NPP registered by I. Maniu and G. Iunian RCP. Along with setting the dates of the parliamentary elections were also set the dates for the elections to the district and public councils. In particular, they had to be held on February 25, 1938, in all districts of Bukovyna and Bessarabia and in the other 13 districts of Moldova, thus covering the north-eastern part of the country. The elections in 21 districts of the south-eastern part and center were scheduled for March 13. The elections in 22 counties in the western part of the country were scheduled

[17](1938). Armată română. Un interview al d-lui general I.Antonescu, ministrul apărării naţionale, acordat ziarului "Giornale d'Italia." *Universul, 21 Ianuarie, Nr.20*, p.1. [Romanian army. An interview by Mr. I. Antonescu, Minister of National Defense, to the newspaper "Giornale d'Italia". *The Universe, January 21, No. 20*, p.1].

for March 20. The council elections in 23 municipalities were set for March 22 and the elections in resident cities were set for the same date[18].

On January 25, 1938, the Council of Ministers at its meeting had to discuss the situation on the parliament meeting and the start of the election campaign. At the same time, several requirements were set for the election process, which limited the ability of political parties in the election campaign. At the same time, it prohibited state and civil servants, priests, and teachers to participate in the propaganda campaign. The rights and capabilities of the police and gendarmerie were expanded. The government continued the tradition of the previous period and directed efforts to find allies among national minorities. At least, an agreement was concluded twice (December 1937 and January 1938) with the German minority, which at the end of March was seen as unfulfilled promises. On the background of the Third Reich struggle for the rights of the German minority in Central Europe and the Anschluss and the plebiscite in Austria the publication in *Franckfurter Zeitung* regarding the violation of the rights of Germans in Romania, was not surprising. The situation was solved at the level of the Ministry of Foreign Affairs, and Minister N. Petrescu-Comnen had to act in terms of proof of equality between Romanian citizens of all nationalities. The press said about the need not to make mistakes in relations between nations[19].

At the same time, a decision to satisfy the population and create the authority of the government was made. In particular, it was an issue of cheaper consumer goods (salt, kerosene, cotton fabrics, tobacco) and the establishment of monopoly on selling them to peasants. Also, from March 1, 1938, they were going to abolish the old tax on peasant ownership and replace it with a tax on goods sold. Tariffs for Romanian Railways in the 3rd class were reduced by 25%. In order to provide foreseen actions of

---

[18](1938). Corpurile legiuitoare au fost dizolvate. *Universul, 21 Ianuarie, Nr. 20*, p.1-2; (1938). Ordinea depunerii listelor. *Universul, 21 Ianuarie, Nr. 20*, p.5; (1938). S'a fixat date alegerilor judeţene şi comunale. *Universul, 22 Ianuarie, Nr. 21*, p.5. [Legitimate bodies were dissolved. *The Universe, January 21, 20*, p.1-2; (1938). The order of submission of the lists. *The Universe, January 21, 20*, p.5; (1938). Date of county and communal elections was set. *The Universe, January 22, Nr. 21*, p.5].

[19](1938). Plângerile minorităţii germane. *Universul, 14 Aprilie, Nr. 103*, p.5. [Complaints of the German minority. *The Universe, April 14, 103*, p.5].

employees the system of remuneration was changed. In the capital, the general mayor C. Breescu announced the reduction of prices for consumer goods. The use of paramilitary formations, including squads of lunchiers was an additional incentive for victory in elections. However, in a number of cases, their presence, even at the meetings of local NGO organizations, could lead to clashes. In early February, similar cases have occurred in the community of Comănești, the towns of Moinești, Ploiești, Adjud, Chernivtsi, and in Ilfov district. In the town of Năsăud the prefect made bribery of voters having sold out 12,000 kg of cotton in order to ensure next voting for the government party. Similar actions compelled the interior minister to make a relative decision and to take harsh actions to make order that did not exclude arrests of the NCP members[20].

The position of the government was discussed in the report of its chairman on occasion of the month of the government's activity on the radio. In particular, it said about the need of the government leader report. The government task was called the realization of Rominism. It became a means against spreading foreigners who penetrated into the political life of Romania. The role of the king who was to become the judge of the mood of the people and his statement about the national needs, which forced the king to bring an active government to power, was also noted. The government was told that it needed time necessary for reforms. The task of the state was to solve the "Jewish issue." O. Goga also called the government a guarantor of the test on nationalism speaking about the awakening of the people and their revival. He recognized the opposition and sabotage to the government activities. In his speech, he argued that Romania included national minorities to the state adhering to their rights and freedoms. He also called for the next parliamentary elections and the need for constructing the national Christian state. He expressed belief in the Romanian people, their will and firm opinion[21].

---

[20]Nedelcu, F. (1973). *Viața politică din România în preajma instaurării dictaturii regale*. Cluj: Dacia, p.230-235. [*Political life in Romania near the establishment of royal dictatorship*. Cluj: Dacia, p.230-235].

[21](1938). Cuvântarea ţinută la Radio de d. Octavian Goga, preşedintele consiliului de miniştri. *Universul, 8 Februarie, Nr. 38*, p. 6. [The speech given to Radio by Mr. Octavian Goga, the chairman of the council of ministers. *The Universe, February 8, Nr. 38*, p.].

Following the report, the manifesto of the government to the country was published and it confirmed Romania being in the state of great changes that led to the National Revolution. The manifesto emphasized the need for elections, demonstrated the measures that had made the country Romanian, made cheaper living conditions. However, the program of government activities, that included preserving the Orthodox Church, the protection of the church marriage, was also announced the manifesto. Other churches should also be placed on the service of the state and the prosperity of the Romanian monarchy glorification. Particular attention should be paid to rural schools providing education in the field of practical agricultural knowledge. They promised to expand the organization of medical institutions in the rural area. It was also necessary to fight tuberculosis, malaria, and rheumatism.

In the economic sphere, the government proclaimed the need for raising agriculture including the supply of farms with agricultural machinery, the establishment of comparable prices for agricultural and industrial products, the proper completion of an agrarian reform. It was important to facilitate the access of foreign capital to Romania for the development of industry. In the area of administration, the government set the task to manage for the sake of securing higher national interests and correcting past mistakes. Foreign policy seemed to be stable because it was promised in the manifesto to carry out foreign policy within existing unions and agreements. Yet the manifesto was a call to participate in the elections and the government launched an election campaign that had not been carried out due to the further change of power[22].

On January 16, 1938, the meeting of the Democratic Union, the Alliance of Democrats (C. Popovici), MADOSZ, RCP, Syndicates and the NPJ of the Galben sector of Bucharest was held, where the participants discussed the prospects of the elections and decided to follow joint electoral roll on February 6, 1938. The delegation of the Democratic Union including A. Joja, V. Bigu, B. Rădulescu, met with I. Maniu and discussed the issue of the fight against the Iron Guard. Meanwhile, on February 9,

---

[22](1938). Manifestul guvernului către țară. *Universul, 8 Februarie, Nr. 38*,p. 6. [Manifesto of the government to the country. *The Universe, February 8, Nr. 38*, p. 6].

1938, O. Goga and C.Z. Codreanu met at I. Gigurtu's house and the parties agreed on the joint electoral roll[23].

The governmental actions caused a crisis in the country, which was explained by the presence of representatives of different groups in the government. At the beginning of February 1938, C.I.C. Brătianu offered the king to establish a coalition government to appease the spirit and stabilize the situation in the country. Yet the government of O. Goga suffered a sudden blow, because on February 8, due to the inability to work in the government, A. Călinescu and I. Gigurtu resigned. On February 10, the king demanded from the chairman of the Council of Ministers to create a government of a "national union." Actually then A. Averescu stated that he was at the king's service. C.I.C. Brătianu and I. Maniu offered to participate in the government as the ministers in no charge, an attempt to save O.Goga as head of government. If A. Văitoianu, C. Angelescu, Gh. Tătărescu had a possibility to join that government, then I. Maniu said that the only possible decision could be formation of the national-peasant government[24].

On February 11, 1938, the order on establishing a state of siege in the country was issued. According to the order, the full authority at the local level was handed over to the commanders of military garrisons. At the same time, the responsibility of the citizens for non-fulfillment of the Council of Ministers or the Ministry of Internal Affairs' orders was strengthened[25]. While analyzing the new government coming to power the

---

[23]Scurtu, I. (1983). *Din viața politică a României (1926-1947): Studiu critic privind istoria Partidului Național-Țărănesc*. București: Editura științifică și enciclopedică, p. 397-398. [*From the Political Life of Romania (1926-1947): Critical Study on the History of the National Peasant Party*. Bucharest: Scientific and Encyclopedic Publishing House, pp. 397-398].

[24]Scurtu, I. (1983). *Din viața politică a României (1926-1947): Studiu critic privind istoria Partidului Național-Țărănesc*. București: Editura științifică și enciclopedică, p. 398-400; Nedelcu, F. (1973). *Viața politică din România în preajma instaurării dictaturii regale*. Cluj: Dacia, p.237-238. [*From the political life of Romania (1926-1947): Critical study on the history of the National Peasant Party*. Bucharest: Scientific and Encyclopedic Publishing House, pp. 398-400; Nedelcu, F. (1973). *Political life in Romania near the establishment of royal dictatorship*. Cluj: Dacia, p. 237-238].

[25]Decretul-lege pentru introducerea stării de asediu //Scurtu I., Mocanu C., Smârcea D. Documente privind istoria României între anii 1918-1944 /Coord. IoanScurtu. - București: editura didactică și pedagogică, R.A., 1995. - P. 439. [Decree-law on the introduction of the siege state // Scurtu I., Mocanu C., Smârcea D. Documents on the history of Romania

police noted at first the appearance of concern in certain circles at the beginning of the government's activities. However, there was a division in society and a significant part of citizens were perceived as those who wanted the order. The representatives of NPP, NCP, "Everything for the country" Party who did not perceive the government's actions in the field of bringing order were considered the opponents of the order[26]. As of March 1938, according to police information in the Storojineţ and Rădăuţi districts in Bukovyna, as well as Baja district, the actions of the government were taken positively, and the peasants noted the order after the dissolution of the parties. At the same time, the former NCP members in Bukovyna expressed their opinion on the possibility of establishing a regime of right-wing radical organization and noted that the Cuza and Goga alliance could be the best for such governing, since their party was a fan of the dynasty. Some dissatisfaction was expressed with the existence of the rights of national minorities and, in particular, the alleged advantages of the Jews, the change in the course of the NCP government, which was generally made by representatives of right-wing radical organizations, as the former chairman of the NCP in Câmpulung district T. Prokopchuk[27].

In general, the short-term activities of the O. Goga government demonstrated the efforts of the National Christian Party representatives to act within the framework of the traditional parliamentary system. This was proved by the government activities, which acted according to the usual scheme of the previous governments replacing the local authorities in the conditions of preparation for new elections. The parliament was considered a means of legalizing the steps of the government. At the same time, the government itself interpreted its steps as disadvantageous to the certain groups of the Romanian society, which led, according to the statements of

---

between 1918-1944 / Coord. IoanScurtu. - Bucharest: didactic and pedagogical publishing house, R.A., 1995. - p. 439].

[26]Arhivele Naţionale ale României (Bucureşti), fond *Direcţia Generală a Poliţiei, 2350, dosar Nr. 3/1938,* fila 13. [National Archives of Romania (Bucharest), fund *Directorate General of Police, 2350, file Nr. 3/1938*, file 13].

[27]Arhivele Naţionale ale României (Bucureşti), fond *Direcţia Generală a Poliţiei, 2350, dosar Nr. 113/1937*, file 73-74, 77. [National Archives of Romania (Bucharest), fund *Directorate General of Police, 2350, file Nr. 113/1937*, file 73-74, 77].

the Council of Ministers head, to the sabotage of individual decisions of the government. The change of the government was a kind of symbolic act, as February 11 became a date that created conditions for the next coming to power of the Hohenzollern-Sigmaringen dynasty.

REFERENCES

Alte două interviewuri ale d-lui prim-ministru Oct. (1938) Goga. [Two other interviews of Prime Minister Oct. Goga]. *Universul, 20 Ianuarie, Nr. 19*, p. 13.

Arhivele Naţionale ale României (Bucureşti), fond *Casa Regală, 727, dosar Nr. 4/1938*. [National Archives of Romania (Bucharest), *Royal House Fund, 727, file Nr. 4/1938*].

Arhivele Naţionale ale României (Bucureşti), fond *Direcţia Generală a Poliţiei, 2350, dosar Nr. 17/1937*. [National Archives of Romania (Bucharest), *fund General Directorate of Police, 2350, file Nr. 17/1937*].

Arhivele Naţionale ale României (Bucureşti), fond *Direcţia Generală a Poliţiei, 2350, dosar Nr. 113/1937*. [National Archives of Romania (Bucharest), *fund General Directorate of Police, 2350, file Nr.113/1937].*

Arhivele Naţionale ale României (Bucureşti), fond *Direcţia Generală a Poliţiei, 2350, dosar Nr. 3/1938*. [National Archives of Romania (Bucharest), *fund General Directorate of Police, 2350, file Nr.3/1938].*

Armată română. (1938). Un interview al d-lui general I.Antonescu, ministrul apărării naţionale, acordat ziarului "Giornale d'Italia." [Romanian army. An interview by Mr. I. Antonescu, Minister of National Defense, to the newspaper "Giornale d'Italia"]. *Universul, 21 Ianuarie, Nr.20*, p.1.

Cenzura presei va trece la Preşedinţia Consiliului. (1938). [The censorship of the press will go to the presidency of the Council]. *Universul, 1 Ianuarie, Nr. 1*, p. 13.

Comercianţi străini cari au firme înscrise după 1930 nu vor putea rămâne în ţară. (1938). [Foreign traders who have companies registered after 1930 will not be able to stay in the country]. *Universul, 21 Ianuarie, Nr. 20*, p.1.

Consiliul de miniştri de Miercuri seara. (1938). [Council of Ministers on Wednesday night]. *Universul, 1 Ianuarie, Nr. 1*, p. 13.

Corpurile legiuitoare au fost dizolvate. (1938). [Legitimate bodies were dissolved].*Universul, 21 Ianuarie, Nr. 20*, p.1-2.

Cuvântarea-program rostită la radio de d. Octavian Goga, preşedinte consiliul de miniştri. (1938). [The radio program spoken by radio by Octavian Goga, chairman of the council of ministers]. *Universul, 3 Ianuarie, Nr. 3*, p. 3.

Cuvântarea ţinută la Radio de d. Octavian Goga, preşedintele consiliului de miniştri. (1938). [The speech given to Radio by Mr. Octavian Goga, the chairman of the council of ministers]. *Universul, 8 Februarie, Nr. 38*, p. 6.

Decretul-lege pentru introducerea stării de asediu. (1995). [Decree-law on the introduction of the siege state]. In I. Scurtu, C. Mocanu, D. Smârcea *Documente privind istoria României între anii 1918-1944* /Coord. Ioan Scurtu. [I. Scurtu, C. Mocanu, D. Smârcea *Documents on the history of Romania between 1918-1944*/Coord. Ioan Scurtu]. (P. 439). Bucureşti: editura didactică şi pedagogică, R.A.

Dizolvarea consiliilor comunale şi judeţene. (1938). [Dissolution of communal and county councils]. *Universul, 1 Ianuarie, Nr. 1*, p. 17.

Instalări de noui prefecţi. 1938). [Installations of new prefects]. *Universul, 1 Ianuarie, Nr. 1*, p.15.

Instalarea nouei comisii interimare a municipiului Timişoara. (1938). [Installing the new Interim Commission of Timisoara]. *Universul, 2 Ianuarie, Nr. 2*, p. 11.

Instalarea noului prefect. (1938). [Installing the new prefect]. *Universul, 3 Ianuarie, Nr.3*, p.2.

Instalarea prefectului de Constanţa. (1938). [Setting up the prefect of Constanta]. *Universul, 3 Ianuarie, Nr.3*, p.2.

Iorga, N. (1939). *Memorii, Vol. VII: Sinuciderea partidelor (1932-1938)*. Bucureşti. [*Memories, Vol. VII: The Suicide of the Parties (1932-1938)*].

La Lugoj. (1938). [At Lugoj]. *Universul, 3 Ianuarie, Nr.3*, p.2.

La Târnava Mare. (1938). [At Târnava Mare].*Universul, 3 Ianuarie, Nr.3*, p.2.

Manifestul guvernului către ţară. (1938). [Manifesto of the government to the country]. *Universul, 8 Februarie, Nr. 38*, p. 6.

Marianne despre Transilvania şi d. Goga... (1938). [Marianne about Transylvania and Mr. Goga ...] *Universul, 21 Ianuarie, Nr. 20*, p. 5.

Nedelcu, F. (1973). *Viaţa politică din România în preajma instaurării dictaturii regale*. [*Political life in Romania near the establishment of royal dictatorship*]. Cluj: Dacia.

Noui comisii interimare comunale judeţene. (1938). [New county interim commission]. *Universul, 21 Ianuarie, Nr. 20*, p. 9.

Noui prefecţi de judeţe. (1938). [The new prefects of counties]. *Universul, 2 Ianuarie, Nr. 2*, p. 5.

Noul prefect al jud. Hunedoara. (1938). [The new prefect of Hunedoara County]. *Universul, 3 Ianuarie, Nr.3*, p.2.

Нове правительство Ґоґа-Куза. (1937). [New government of Goga-Cuza].*Час, 30 грудня, Ч. 2632*.

Ordinea depunerii listelor. (1938). [The order of submission of the lists]. *Universul, 21 Ianuarie, Nr. 20*, p.5.

Pop, Gh.T. (1978). *Caracterul antinaţional şi antipopular al activităţii Partidului Naţional Creştin*. [*The anti-national and antipopular character of the activity of the National Christian Party*]. Cluj-Napoca: Dacia.

Правительство Татареску-Ґоґи.*Час, 29 грудня, Ч. 2631*. (1937). [The government of Tataresc u-Goga. *Times, December 29, Nr. 2631*].

Plângerile minorităţii germane. (1938). [Complaints of the German minority]. *Universul, 14 Aprilie, Nr. 103*, p.5.

Presa străină salută cu satisfacţie noul guvern Goga. (1938). [The foreign press welcomes the new Goga government with satisfaction]. *Universul, 1 Ianuarie, Nr. 1*, p. 8.

Presa străină despre noul guvern Român. (1938). [Foreign press about the new Romanian government]. *Universul, 2 Ianuarie, Nr. 2*, p.8.

Retragerea licenţelor de băuturi spirtoase date evreilor. (1938). [Withdrawal of licenses for spirits given to Jews]. *Universul, 1 Ianuarie, Nr. 1*, p. 17.

Schimbări de prefecţi. (1938). [Changes of prefects]. *Universul, 25 Ianuarie, Nr. 24*, p. 5.

Scurtu, I. (1983).*Din viața politică a României (1926-1947): Studiu critic privind istoria Partidului Național-Țărănesc.* [*From the Political Life of Romania (1926-1947): Critical Study on the History of the National Peasant Party*]. București: Editura științifică și enciclopedică.

Sonea, E., & Sonea, G. (1978).*Viața economică și politică a României. 1933-1938.* [*Romania's economic and political life. 1933-1938*]. București: Editura științifică și enciclopedică.

S'a fixat date alegerilor judeţene şi comunale. (1938). [Date of county and communal elections was set]. *Universul, 22 Ianuarie, Nr. 21*, p.5.

Un început de românizare a presei. (1938). [A beginning of Romanization of the press]. *Universul, 1 Ianuarie, Nr. 1*, p. 13.

Язькова, А.А. (1963). *Румыния накануне Второй мировой войны: 1934-1939 гг.*Москва: изд-во АН СССР. [*Romania on the eve of World War II: 1934-1939*. Moscow: Publishing House of the USSR Academy of Sciences].

Biographical Sketch

IhorPiddubnyi

Affiliation: Faculty of History, Political Sciences and International Relations of Yurii Fedcovich National University at Chernivtsi

Education: PhD in history

Business Address: Mihailo Kotsyubinski str., 2 Chernivtsi 58000 Ukraina

Professional Appointments: Associate Professor of the Department of History of New and Modern Time Yurii Fedcovich National University at Chernivtsi

Publications from the Last 3 Years:

ПіддубнийІ. А. Реформування органів влади та здійснення заходів з уніфікації в умовах авторитарного режиму в Румунії у 1938-1939 рр. (На прикладі Цинуту Сучава) [Reforming of the authorities and implementing unification measures during the authoritarian regime in Romania in 1938-1939 (on the example of Suceava County)] //*Русин.* [Rusin.]- 2015. - № 1.(39) - С. 182-202.

Піддубний І. Організаційний період соціалістичного руху в Румунії (1918-1921 рр.) [Organizational period of the socialist movement in Romania (1918-1921)] //*Science and Education. A new dimension. Hymanities and social sciences*, III (8), Issue: 52, 2015. - P. 18-22.

Ihor Piddubnii (Chernivtsi) *Way of life and living conditions in Chernivtsi (1918-1940)* //https://memoryofvanishedurbanpopulations.wordpress.com/33-2/general-city-history/.

Zatulovskaja, Elena, Igor' Piddubnyj, Marija Ungurjan Die Darstellung des Zweiten Weltkrieges im Heimatmuseum der Stadt Czernowitz/ Cernivci [The demonstration of the Second World War in the Chernivtsi City Museum] //Der zweite Weltkrieg. Kulturtourismus und Politik in Grenzregionen: Dokumentation des internationalen Workshops in Seelow, vom 15. bis 17. April 2015 /*II Wojna Swiatowa. Turystyka kulturowa i polityka w regionach granicznych: Dokumentacja miedzynarodowych warzstatow w Seelow*, 15-17 kwietnia 2015 r. - Frankfurt-am-Oder, 2015. - S.74-77. [*World War II. Cultural tourism and politics in border regions: Documentation of the international workshop in Seelow*, 15 to 17 April 2015].

Піддубний І. “Hrenciuc Daniel Provocările vecinătății. Ucrainenii Bucovineni în Regatul României Mari (1918-1940). Contribuții”

[Review on Hrenciuc Daniel Neighborhood challenges. The Ukrainians of Bucovina in the Kingdom of Great Romania (1918-1940). Contributions.] *//Історична панорама: Збірник наукових статей ЧНУ. Спеціальність "Історія." - Чернівці: Чернівецький нац. ун-т*, 2015. - Вип. 20. - С.128-153 [*Historical panorama: Collection of scientific articles of ChNU. Specialty "History."* - Chernivtsi: Chernivtsi National University, 2015. - Issue 20].

Піддубний І.А. Ліга націонал-християнського захисту у боротьбі за парламентські місця та владу (1926-1933 рр.) [League of National Christian Protection in the struggle for parliamentary seats and power (1926-1933)] *//Гілея. Науковий вісник. Збірник наукових праць. - Вип. 101 (№10): Історичні науки, філософські науки, політичні науки.* - К., 2015. - С. 62-66 [*Gilea. Scientific Herald. Collection of scientific works. - Whip 101 (№10): Historical sciences, philosophical sciences, political sciences.* - Kyiv, 2015].

ПіддубнийІ. "Hrenciuc Daniel Provocările vecinătății. Ucrainenii Bucovineni în Regatul României Mari (1918-1940). Contribuții" [Review on Hrenciuc, Daniel. Neighborhood challenges. The Ukrainians of Bucovina in the Kingdom of Great Romania (1918-1940). Contributions] *//Історична панорама: Збірник наукових статей ЧНУ. Спеціальність "Історія." - Чернівці: Чернівецький нац. ун-т*, 2015. - Вип. 21. - С.112-137 [*Historical panorama: Collection of scientific articles of ChNU. Specialty "History."* - Chernivtsi: Chernivtsi National University, 2015. - Issue 21].

ПіддубнийІ.А. Пріорітети зовнішньополітичної діяльності урядів Румунії у 1918-1940 рр. [The priorities of the Romanian governments' activities in the foreign policy in 1918-1940. *//Зовнішня політика і дипломатія: Український і світовий досвід: збірник тез доповідей* (23 грудня 2015, м.Київ) /за заг.ред. В.Г.Ціватого, Н.О.Татаренко. - К.: ДАУ при МЗС України, 2015. - С.177-179 [*Foreign policy and diplomacy: Ukrainian and world experience: collection of abstracts* (December 23, 2015, Kiev) /under V.G. Tsivatyi, N.O.Tatarenko. - Kyiv, 2015].

ПіддубнийІ. Міське самоуправління міжвоєнного періоду на Буковині (на прикладі муніципії Чернівці) [Municipal self-government of the interwar period in Bukovina (on an example of the Chernivtsi municipality)] //*Влада та управління. Збірник наукових праць.* - Вип.4. - Чернівці: "Букрек," 2016. - С.236-248 [// *Government and administration. Collection of scientific works.* - Issue 4. - Chernivtsi, 2016].

ПіддубнийІ. Націоналістичний студентський рух та формування праворадикальних політичних організацій в Румунії (1919-1925 рр.) [Nationalist Students' Movement and the Formation of Right-Radical Political Organizations in Romania (1919-1925)] //*Наукові записки Тернопільського національного педагогічного університету імені Володимира Гнатюка. Серія: Історія* /За заг. ред. проф. І.С.Зуляка. - Тернопіль: Вид-во ТПНУ ім. В.Гнатюка, 2016. -Вип.1. - Ч.2. - С. 94-101 [*Scientific Papers of the Ternopil National Pedagogical University named after Volodymyr Hnatyuk. Series: History* / Com. Ed. prof. I.S. Zulyaka. - Ternopil: View of TPNU them. V. Gnatyuk, 2016. -V.1 - Part 2].

Piddubnii Ihor Образование, программные положения и деятельность Национал-христианской Партии в Румынии (1935-1938) [Foundation, program principles and activities of the National Christian Party in Romania (1935-1938)] //*Acta Scientifica Academiae Ostroviensis. Sectio A: Nauki Humanistyczne, Społecznei Techniczne.* - 2015. - Nr. 6 (2). - Ostrowiec Świętokryski. - S. 193-205 [*Scientific Journal of Ostrowiec Academy. Section A: The Humanities, Technical and Social Sciences.* - 2015. - Nr. 6 (2)]. http://zn.wsbip.edu.pl/sectioa/zeszyt_2_2015.pdf.

Піддубний І. Урядова діяльність в умовах спроби трансформації політичного режиму в Румунії у 1938-1940 рр. [Government activity during the attempt of transformation of the political regime in Romania in 1938-1940] //*Історична панорама: Науковий збірник ЧНУ. Спеціальність "Історія."* - Чернівці: Чернівецький нац. ун-т, 2016. - Вип. 22-23. - С.96-131 [*Historical panorama: Scientific collection of the CHNU. Specialty "History."* - Chernivtsi: Chernivtsi National University. un-t, 2016. - Issue 22-23].

Піддубний І. Урядова діяльність в умовах спроби трансформації політичного режиму в Румунії у 1938-1940 рр. (закінчення) [Government activity during the attempt of transformation of the political regime in Romania in 1938-1940 (end)] //*Історична панорама: Науковий збірникЧНУ. Спеціальність "Історія."* - Чернівці: Чернівецький нац. ун-т, 2017. - Вип. 24. - С.53-79 [*Historical panorama: Scientific collection of the CHNU. Specialty "History."* - Chernivtsi: Chernivtsi National University. un-t, 2017. - Issue 24].

Піддубний І. Червнева реставрація 1930 р. в Румунії у висвітленні газети "Universul" [June restoration of 1930 in Romania in the coverage of the newspaper "Universul"] //*Науковий вісник Чернівецького національного університету імені Юрія Федьковича: Історія.* - Чернівці: Чернівецький університет, 2017. - №1. - С.82-88 [*Scientific Bulletin of the Chernivtsi National University named after Yuri Fedkovich: History*. - Chernivtsi: Chernivtsi University, 2017. - No. 1].

Піддубний І. Соціал-демократична організація Буковини в загальнорумунському політичному просторі 1920-х - 1930-х років [The Social Democratic Organization of Bukovina in the Romanian political space of the 1920s - 1930s] //*XI буковинська міжнародна історико-краєзнавча конференція присвячена 100-річчю Української Національної революції. Тези доповідей* (Чернівці, 20-21 жовтня 2017 р.). - Чернівці: Технодрук, 2017. - С.36-37. [*The XI Bukovinian International Historical and Local History Conference dedicated to the 100th anniversary of the Ukrainian National Revolution.* Abstracts (Chernivtsi, October 20-21, 2017). - Chernivtsi: Technodruk, 2017].

Піддубний І.А. Перша світова війна та революційні події 1917-1918 рр. як фактор реалізації ідеї створення "Великої Румунії" [First World War and revolutionary events of 1917-1918 as a factor for realizing the idea of the creation of "Great Romania"]//*Вісник*

Черкаського університету. Серія історичні науки. 2017 рік. - Черкаси, 2017. - №1. - С.42-49 [*Bulletin of the Cherkasy University. Series of historical sciences.* 2017].

Piddubnyj Iğor Černivci u međuratnom razdoblju [Chernivtsi during the interwar period] //*Bukovina Буковина: Prijevodi s ukrajinskoga* /Prizedili Jevgenij Paščenko, Tetyana Fuderer. - Zagreb, 2017. - S. 135 -146. Chernivals in the Intermediate Period [*Bukovina Bukovina: Translations from the Ukrainian* / Trans. Eugen Paschchenko, Tetyana Fuderer. - Zagreb, 2017].

ПіддубнийІ. Театральне життя Буковини у міжвоєнний період [Bukovinian theatrical life during the interwar period] //Вісник центру буковинознавства. Збірник наукових праць науково-дослідного Центру буковинознавства Чернівецького національного університету імені Юрія Федьковича. - Чернівці: Технодрук, 2017. - Т.1. - С.104 - 126 [*Bulletin of the Center of Bukovina Studies*. Collection of scientific works of the Research Center of Bukovina Studies of Chernivtsi National University named after Yuri Fedkovich. - Chernivtsi: Technodruk, 2017.]

BIBLIOGRAPHY

Alexandre Safran and the Jews of Romania during the installation of the communist regime: newly discovered documents from the American and British diplomatic archives (1944-1948)

LCCN	2018380125
Type of material	Book
Uniform title	Alexandre Safran et les juifs de Roumanie durant l'instauration du communisme. English
Main title	Alexandre Safran and the Jews of Romania during the installation of the communist regime: newly discovered documents from the American and British diplomatic archives (1944-1948) / [edited by] Carol Iancu, honorary member of the Romanian Academy; translated by Felicia Waldman; foreword, Professor Alexandru Zub, member of the Romanian Academy.
Published/Produced	Iaşi: Editura Universităţii "Alexandru Ioan Cuza", 2018.
Description	553 pages: illustrations, portraits, facsimiles; 24 cm.
ISBN	9786067144239 6067144239

LC classification	BM755.S223 A4413 2018
Related names	Iancu, Carol, editor.
	Zub, Al., writer of foreword.
	Waldman, Felicia, 1969- translator.
Subjects	Safran, Alexandre.
	Iancu, Carol--Bibliography.
	Iancu, Carol.
	Safran, Alexandre.
	1900-1999
	Rabbis--Romania--Biography--Sources.
	Rabbis--Switzerland--Biography--Sources.
	Jews--Romania--History--20th century--Sources.
Notes	Includes bibliographical references and indexes.
	"By the same author [Carol Iancu]": pages 5-8.
	Documents chiefly in English, some in French or Romanian; editorial matter in English.
Series	Colecția Historica. Seria Dagesh; 8
	Colecția Historica. Seria Dagesh; 8.

Ambiguous transitions: gender, the state, and everyday life in socialist and postsocialist Romania

LCCN	2018000867
Type of material	Book
Personal name	Massino, Jill, author.
Main title	Ambiguous transitions: gender, the state, and everyday life in socialist and postsocialist Romania / Jill M. Massino.
Edition	1st Edition.
Published/Produced	New York: Berghahn Books, [2018]
Description	1 online resource.
ISBN	9781785335990 (eBook)
LC classification	HQ1075.5.R6
Contents	The times, they are a changin': gender, citizenship, and the transition to socialism --

Children of the revolution: gender, and the (ab)normality of growing up socialist -- Career opportunities: gender, work, and identity -- Love and marriage: gender and the transformation of marital roles and relations -- It's a family affair: motherhood, reproductive politics, and state welfare -- Good times, bad times: gender, consumption, and lifestyle -- Revolution blues: gender and the transformation from socialism to pluarlism -- Bibliography -- Index.

Subjects Gender identity--Romania.
Women--Romania--Social conditions.
Women and communism--Romania--History.
Romania--History--1944-1989.
Romania--History--1989-

Notes Includes bibliographical references and index.

Additional formats Print version: Massino, Jill, author. Ambiguous transitions 1st Edition. New York: Berghahn Books, [2018] 9781785335983 (DLC) 2017052489

Ambiguous transitions: gender, the state, and everyday life in socialist and postsocialist Romania

LCCN 2017052489

Type of material Book

Personal name Massino, Jill, author.

Main title Ambiguous transitions: gender, the state, and everyday life in socialist and postsocialist Romania / Jill M. Massino.

Edition 1st Edition.

Published/Produced New York: Berghahn Books, [2018]

ISBN 9781785335983 (hardback: alk. paper)

LC classification HQ1075.5.R6 M37 2018

Contents The times, they are a changin': gender,

	citizenship, and the transition to socialism -- Children of the revolution: gender, and the (ab)normality of growing up socialist -- Career opportunities: gender, work, and identity -- Love and marriage: gender and the transformation of marital roles and relations -- It's a family affair: motherhood, reproductive politics, and state welfare -- Good times, bad times: gender, consumption, and lifestyle -- Revolution blues: gender and the transformation from socialism to pluarlism -- Bibliography -- Index.
Subjects	Gender identity--Romania. Women--Romania--Social conditions. Women and communism--Romania--History. Romania--History--1944-1989. Romania--History--1989-
Notes	Includes bibliographical references and index.
Additional formats	Online version: Massino, Jill, author. Ambiguous transitions 1st Edition. New York: Berghahn Books, [2018] 9781785335990 (DLC) 2018000867

America's first spy: the tragic heroism of Frank Wisner

LCCN	2018027336
Type of material	Book
Personal name	Maior, George Cristian, author.
Main title	America's first spy: the tragic heroism of Frank Wisner / George Cristian Maior.
Published/Produced	London; Washington, DC: Academica Press, [2018]
ISBN	9781680530728
LC classification	UB271.U52 W576 2018
Portion of title	Tragic heroism of Frank Wisner
Summary	"Romanian diplomat and scholar George Cristian

Maior - currently serving as Romania's ambassador in Washington - recounts the thrilling tale of America's first spy drama - the legendary Frank Wisner's intelligence operations in Romania as World War II ended and the Cold War dawned. An Office of Strategic Services operative who later rose to become the Central Intelligence Agency's operations chief before his tragic suicide, Wisner's mission bestrode two worlds and witnessed profound changes that global politics have grappled with ever since."--Provided by publisher.

Contents Last waltz for Bucharest -- The boy from Laurel -- The detachment -- Lawyers, bankers and spies -- The maiden mission -- Boo hoo, baby. I'm no spy -- Into the quicksand -- Bucharest - The little Paris -- Hammerhead -- A spy is born -- The dawn of the Cold War -- Goodbye, Romania! -- Among the ruins -- Back in business -- Gentlemen-rankers -- Locust Hill Farm and the Sunday night suppers -- The mighty Wurlitzer -- Displaced persons camps -- A lot of money and even more luck -- The CIA vs. the world -- The Red Scare -- The downfall -- Epilogue.

Subjects Wisner, Frank, 1909-1965.
United States. Office of Strategic Services--Officials and employees--Biography.
United States. Central Intelligence Agency--Officials and employees--Biography.
Intelligence officers--United States--Biography.
Spies--United States--Biography
Espionage--Romania--History--20th century.
Intelligence service--United States--History--20th century.

	Espionage, American--History--20th century.
	Cold War.
Notes	Includes bibliographical references and index.

Angela Gheorghiu: a life for art

LCCN	2018023843
Type of material	Book
Personal name	Gheorghiu, Angela, author.
Main title	Angela Gheorghiu: a life for art / Angela Gheorghiu with Jon Tolansky.
Published/Produced	Lebanon, NH: ForeEdge, [2018]
ISBN	9781611689129 (cloth)
LC classification	ML420.G379 A3 2018
Related names	Tolansky, Jon.
Subjects	Gheorghiu, Angela.
	Sopranos (Singers)--Romania--Biography.
Form/Genre	Autobiographies.
Notes	Includes bibliographical references and index.
Additional formats	Online version: Gheorghiu, Angela, author. Angela Gheorghiu Lebanon, NH: ForeEdge, [2018] 9781512603071 (DLC) 2018025317

Angela Gheorghiu: a life for art

LCCN	2018025317
Type of material	Book
Personal name	Gheorghiu, Angela, author.
Main title	Angela Gheorghiu: a life for art / Angela Gheorghiu with Jon Tolansky.
Published/Produced	Lebanon, NH: ForeEdge, [2018]
Description	1 online resource.
ISBN	9781512603071 (epub, pdf, & mobi)
LC classification	ML420.G379
Related names	Tolansky, Jon.
Subjects	Gheorghiu, Angela.

Sopranos (Singers)--Romania--Biography.

Form/Genre Autobiographies.

Notes Includes bibliographical references and index.

Additional formats Print version: Gheorghiu, Angela, author. Angela Gheorghiu Lebanon, NH: ForeEdge, [2018] 9781611689129 (DLC) 2018023843

Beet juice buddies

LCCN 2018013844

Type of material Book

Personal name Hoena, B. A., author.

Main title Beet juice buddies / by Blake Hoena; illustrated by Dave Bardin.

Published/Produced North Mankato, Minnesota: Stone Arch Books, a Capstone imprint, [2018]
©2019

ISBN 9781496564160 (hardcover)
9781496564207 (pbk.)

LC classification PZ7.H67127 Be 2018

Related names Bardin, Dave (Illustrator), illustrator.

Summary Mina the vampire and her family are on vacation in Transylvania, and Mina has two problems--she has to conceal the fact that she prefers beet juice to blood when she meets great-great-great grandpa Drac, and she needs to rescue a group of tourists who do not realize that they are on the dinner menu.

Subjects Vampires--Juvenile fiction.
Monsters--Juvenile fiction.
Heroes--Juvenile fiction.
Vampires--Fiction.
Monsters--Fiction.
Heroes--Fiction.
Transylvania (Romania)--Juvenile fiction.

	Transylvania (Romania)--Fiction.
	Romania--Fiction.
Additional formats	Online version: Hoena, B. A., author. Beet juice buddies North Mankato, Minnesota: Stone Arch Books, a Capstone imprint, [2018] 9781496564245 (DLC) 2018016940
Series	Monster heroes
	Hoena, B. A. Monster heroes.

Beet juice buddies

LCCN	2018016940
Type of material	Book
Personal name	Hoena, B. A., author.
Main title	Beet juice buddies / by Blake Hoena; illustrated by Dave Bardin.
Published/Produced	North Mankato, Minnesota: Stone Arch Books, a Capstone imprint, [2018]
	©2019
Description	1 online resource.
ISBN	9781496564245 (eBook PDF)
LC classification	PZ7.H67127
Related names	Bardin, Dave (Illustrator), illustrator.
Summary	Mina the vampire and her family are on vacation in Transylvania, and Mina has two problems--she has to conceal the fact that she prefers beet juice to blood when she meets great-great-great grandpa Drac, and she needs to rescue a group of tourists who do not realize that they are on the dinner menu.
Subjects	Vampires--Juvenile fiction.
	Monsters--Juvenile fiction.
	Heroes--Juvenile fiction.
	Vampires--Fiction.
	Monsters--Fiction.

	Heroes--Fiction.
	Transylvania (Romania)--Juvenile fiction.
	Transylvania (Romania)--Fiction.
	Romania--Fiction.
Additional formats	Print version: Hoena, B. A., author. Beet juice buddies North Mankato, Minnesota: Stone Arch Books, a Capstone imprint, [2018] 9781496564160 (DLC) 2018013844
Series	Monster heroes

Bright we burn

LCCN	2017045647
Type of material	Book
Personal name	White, Kiersten, author.
Main title	Bright we burn / Kiersten White.
Edition	First edition.
Published/Produced	New York: Delacorte Press, [2018]
Description	389 pages: map; 24 cm.
ISBN	9780553522396 (hc)
	9780553522402 (glb)
LC classification	PZ7.W583764 Br 2018
Summary	To build the country she wants, Lada, the brutal ruler of Wallachia, must destroy everything that came before, including her relationships with brother Radu and former love Mehmed, Sultan of the Ottoman Empire.
Subjects	Princesses--Fiction.
	Good and evil--Fiction.
	Transylvania (Romania)--History--15th century--Fiction.
	Istanbul (Turkey)--History--15th century--Fiction.
	Turkey--History--Mehmed II, 1451-1481--Fiction.
Notes	Sequel to: Now I rise.

Debating migration as a public problem: national publics and transnational fields

LCCN	2018002350
Type of material	Book
Main title	Debating migration as a public problem: national publics and transnational fields / edited by Camelia Beciu [and three others].
Published/Produced	New York: Peter Lang, [2018]
ISBN	9781433155482 (pbk.: alk. paper) 9781433155345 (hardback: alk. paper)
LC classification	HD8378.5.A2 D395 2018
Related names	Beciu, Camelia, 1967- editor.
Subjects	Foreign workers--Government policy--European Union countries. Foreign workers--Government policy--Romania--Case studies. European Union countries--Emigration and immigration--Government policy. Romania--Emigration and immigration--Government policy--Case studies.
Notes	Includes bibliographical references and index.
Series	Global crises and the media, 1947-2587; volume 24

Holocaust public memory in postcommunist Romania

LCCN	2017040235
Type of material	Book
Main title	Holocaust public memory in postcommunist Romania / edited by Alexandru Florian.
Published/Produced	Bloomington, Indiana: Indiana University Press, [2018] ©2018
Description	xxxi, 291 pages; 24 cm.
ISBN	9780253032706 (hardback: alk. paper)

	9780253032713 (pbk.: alk. paper)
LC classification	DS135.R7 H645 2018
Related names	Florian, Alexandru, editor.
Subjects	Holocaust, Jewish (1939-1945)--Romania--Historiography. Romania--Ethnic relations.
Notes	Includes bibliographical references and index.
Additional formats	Online version: Holocaust public memory in postcommunist Romania Bloomington, Indiana: Indiana University Press, [2018] 9780253032744 (DLC) 2017041142
Series	Studies in antisemitism

Hungarian religion, Romanian blood: a minority's struggle for national belonging, 1920-1945

LCCN	2017051213
Type of material	Book
Personal name	Davis, R. Chris (Robert Chris), 1975- author.
Main title	Hungarian religion, Romanian blood: a minority's struggle for national belonging, 1920-1945 / R. Chris Davis.
Published/Produced	Madison, Wisconsin: The University of Wisconsin Press, [2018] ©2018
ISBN	9780299316402 (cloth: alk. paper)
LC classification	DR214.C73 D38 2018
Summary	Amid the rising nationalism and racial politics that culminated in World War II, European countries wishing to "purify" their nations often forced unwanted populations to migrate. The targeted minorities had few options, but as Chris Davis shows, they sometimes used creative tactics to fight back, redefining their identities to serve their own interests. Davis's highly illuminating

	example is the case of the little-known Csangos, an ethnic community in Moldavian Romania who practice Catholicism and speak a mix of Hungarian and Romanian. Romania wanted to expel them; Hungary wanted them for resettlement. Aided by Catholic priests, the Csangos resisted deportation with a concerted strategy involving blood samples, anthropologists, and historians, hoping to exempt themselves from the discrimination and violence that targeted Jews, Roma, Slavs, and other minorities. Davis draws on many facets of the Csangos' refashioning to add insight to debates about racial politics, national communities, and ethnic and religious minorities past and present.
Subjects	Csangos--Romania--Moldavia--History--20th century. Moldavia (Romania)--Ethnic relations--20th century.
Notes	Includes bibliographical references and index.

Inside the East European planned economy: state planning, factory and manager

LCCN	2017054007
Type of material	Book
Personal name	Sucala, Voicu Ion, author.
Main title	Inside the East European planned economy: state planning, factory and manager / Voicu Ion Sucala.
Edition	First Edition.
Published/Produced	New York: Routledge, 2018.
ISBN	9781138068681 (hardback)
LC classification	HC405 .S83 2018
Contents	Introduction -- Organisation, power and politics

	in the communist regime -- Romanian industrialisation: legal frame, characteristics and social consequences -- Methodology -- Plan and enterprise in communist Romania -- The human side of the communist enterprise -- Conclusions -- Appendix 1. List of archival documents -- Appendix 2. List of participants -- Index.
Subjects	Industrial management--Romania. Romania--Economic policy--1945-1989. Romania--Politics and government--1944-1989.
Notes	Includes bibliographical references and index.
Series	BASEES/Routledge series on Russian and East European studies; 122

Integrity in the legal, educational and private environment = L'intégrité dans le secteur juridique, éducatif et privé = Integrität im rechtlichen, akademischen und privaten Umfeld

LCCN	2018399306
Type of material	Book
Main title	Integrity in the legal, educational and private environment = L'intégrité dans le secteur juridique, éducatif et privé = Integrität im rechtlichen, akademischen und privaten Umfeld / Rodica Aida Popa (coordonator) [and seven others].
Published/Produced	Bucureşti: Editura C.H. Beck, 2018.
Description	385 pages; 24 cm
ISBN	9786061807673
LC classification	KKR1610 .I584 2018
Parallel title	Intégrité dans le secteur juridique, éducatif et privé Integrität im rechtlichen, akademischen und privaten Umfeld
Related names	Popa, Rodica Aida, editor.

Subjects	Judges--Romania. Judicial ethics--Romania. Political questions and judicial power--Romania. Justice, Administration of--Romania. Political corruption--Prevention. Integrity.
Notes	Includes bibliographical references. English, French, and German.

Mathematics almost everywhere: in memory of Solomon Marcus

LCCN	2018011303
Type of material	Book
Main title	Mathematics almost everywhere: in memory of Solomon Marcus / editors, Alexandra Bello, Northwestern University, USA, Cristian S. Calude, University of Auckland, New Zealand, Tudor Zamfirescu, Technical University of Dortmund, Germany, "Simion Stoilow" Mathematical Institute of the Roumanian Academy, Roumania.
Published/Produced	New Jersey: World Scientific, 2018.
Description	xix, 231 pages: illustrations; 24 cm
ISBN	9789813237308 (hardcover: alk. paper)
LC classification	QA29.M3565 M38 2018
Related names	Bellow, A. (Alexandra), 1935- editor. Calude, Cristian, 1952- editor. Zamfirescu, Tudor, editor.
Subjects	Marcus, Solomon. Mathematicians--Romania. Mathematical linguistics. Mathematical analysis. Festschriften.
Notes	Includes bibliographical references and index.

My life as a spy: investigations in a secret police file

LCCN	2017047454
Type of material	Book
Personal name	Verdery, Katherine, 1948- author.
Main title	My life as a spy: investigations in a secret police file / Katherine Verdery.
Published/Produced	Durham: Duke University Press, 2018.
Description	xvi, 323 pages: illustrations; 24 cm
ISBN	9780822370666 (hardcover: alk. paper) 9780822370819 (pbk.: alk. paper)
LC classification	HV8241.8.A45 V47 2018
Contents	The 1970s: "the folklorist" as military spy -- The 1980s: the enemy's many masks -- Excursus: reflections on reading one's file -- Rcvclation -- Ruminations.
Subjects	Verdery, Katherine, 1948- Romania. Securitatea--History--Sources. Cold War--Personal narratives. Secret service--Romania--History--20th century--Sources. Romania--Politics and government--20th century--Sources.
Notes	Includes bibliographical references and index.
Additional formats	Online version: Verdery, Katherine, 1948- author. My life as a spy Durham: Duke University Press, 2018 9780822371908 (DLC) 2017052453

Patrick Leigh Fermor: noble encounters between Budapest and Transylvania

LCCN	2018022873
Type of material	Book
Personal name	O'Sullivan, Michael, 1957- author.
Main title	Patrick Leigh Fermor: noble encounters between Budapest and Transylvania / Michael O'Sullivan.

Published/Produced	Budapest; New York: Central European University Press, 2018. ©2018
Description	1 online resource.
ISBN	9789633861721 (pdf)
LC classification	DB955.6.F47
Summary	"Patrick Leigh Fermor: Noble Encounters Between Budapest and Transylvania is the extraordinary story of how one unknown young man charmed his way into the castles, manor houses, beds and lives of some of the most influential people in a part of the former Austro-Hungarian Empire which was then on the cusp of tremendous change. This book records the history of a class, as witnessed by an exceptional young outsider in 1934 and also records what happened to many of them once the grim reality of Communism took hold in this part of East-Central Europe. It is also a portrait of Budapest in 1934, a grand city about to change forever."-- Provided by the publisher.
Contents	Budapest -- Across the Alföld: The Great Hungarian Plain -- The Banat -- Transylvania.
Subjects	Fermor, Patrick Leigh--Travel--Hungary. Fermor, Patrick Leigh--Travel--Romania--Transylvania. Hungary--Description and travel. Transylvania (Romania)--Description and travel. Hungary--Social life and customs--20th century. Transylvania (Romania)--Social life and customs--20th century.
Notes	Includes bibliographical references and index.
Additional formats	Print version: O'Sullivan, Michael, 1957- author. Patrick Leigh Fermor Budapest; New York:

Central European University Press, 2018 9786155225642 (DLC) 2018009070

Patrick Leigh Fermor: noble encounters between Budapest and Transylvania

LCCN	2018009070
Type of material	Book
Personal name	O'Sullivan, Michael, 1957- author.
Main title	Patrick Leigh Fermor: noble encounters between Budapest and Transylvania / Michael O'Sullivan.
Published/Produced	Budapest; New York: Central European University Press, 2018. ©2018
ISBN	9786155225642 (pbk.: alk. paper)
LC classification	DB955.6.F47 O88 2018
Summary	"Patrick Leigh Fermor: Noble Encounters Between Budapest and Transylvania is the extraordinary story of how one unknown young man charmed his way into the castles, manor houses, beds and lives of some of the most influential people in a part of the former Austro-Hungarian Empire which was then on the cusp of tremendous change. This book records the history of a class, as witnessed by an exceptional young outsider in 1934 and also records what happened to many of them once the grim reality of Communism took hold in this part of East-Central Europe. It is also a portrait of Budapest in 1934, a grand city about to change forever."-- Provided by the publisher.
Contents	Budapest -- Across the Alföld: The Great Hungarian Plain -- The Banat -- Transylvania.
Subjects	Fermor, Patrick Leigh--Travel--Hungary. Fermor, Patrick Leigh--Travel--Romania--

Transylvania.
Hungary--Description and travel.
Transylvania (Romania)--Description and travel.
Hungary--Social life and customs--20th century.
Transylvania (Romania)--Social life and customs--20th century.

Notes Includes bibliographical references and index.

Additional formats Online version: O'Sullivan, Michael, 1957- author. Patrick Leigh Fermor Budapest; New York: Central European University Press, 2018 9789633861721 (DLC) 2018022873

Physicians, peasants and modern medicine: imagining rurality in Romania, 1860-1910

LCCN 2018029611

Type of material Book

Personal name Bărbulescu, Constantin, 1969- author.

Uniform title România medicilor. English

Main title Physicians, peasants and modern medicine: imagining rurality in Romania, 1860-1910 / by Constantin Barbulescu.

Published/Produced Budapest: New York: Central European University Press, [2018]

Description 1 online resource.

ISBN 9789633862681 ()

LC classification RA771.7.R6

Portion of title Imagining rurality in Romania, 1860-1910

Subjects Rural health--Romania--History--19th century.
Rural health--Romania--History--20th century.
Medicine, Rural--Romania--History--19th century.
Medicine, Rural--Romania--History--20th century.
Social medicine--Romania--History--19th

century.
Social medicine--Romania--History--20th century.

Notes Includes bibliographical references and index.

Additional formats Online version: Bărbulescu, Constantin, 1969- author. Physicians, peasants and modern medicine Budapest: New York: Central European University Press, [2018] 9789633862681 (DLC) 2018029609
Print version: Bărbulescu, Constantin, 1969- author. Physicians, peasants and modern medicine Budapest: New York: Central European University Press, [2018] 9789633862674 (DLC) 2018026384

Series CEU Press studies in the history of medicine; volume XII

Physicians, peasants and modern medicine: imagining rurality in Romania, 1860-1910

LCCN 2018029609

Type of material Book

Personal name Bărbulescu, Constantin, 1969- author.

Uniform title România medicilor. English

Main title Physicians, peasants and modern medicine: imagining rurality in Romania, 1860-1910 / by Constantin Barbulescu.

Published/Produced Budapest: New York: Central European University Press, [2018]

Description 1 online resource.

ISBN 9789633862681 ()

LC classification RA771.7.R6

Portion of title Imagining rurality in Romania, 1860-1910

Subjects Rural health--Romania--History--19th century.
Rural health--Romania--History--20th century.

	Medicine, Rural--Romania--History--19th century.
	Medicine, Rural--Romania--History--20th century.
	Social medicine--Romania--History--19th century.
	Social medicine--Romania--History--20th century.
Notes	Includes bibliographical references and index.
Additional formats	Print version: Bărbulescu, Constantin, 1969- author. Physicians, peasants and modern medicine Budapest: New York: Central European University Press, [2018] 9789633862674 (DLC) 2018026384
Series	CEU Press studies in the history of medicine; volume XII

Physicians, peasants and modern medicine: imagining rurality in Romania, 1860-1910

LCCN	2018026384
Type of material	Book
Personal name	Bărbulescu, Constantin, 1969- author.
Uniform title	România medicilor. English
Main title	Physicians, peasants and modern medicine: imagining rurality in Romania, 1860-1910 / by Constantin Barbulescu.
Published/Produced	Budapest: New York: Central European University Press, [2018]
ISBN	9789633862674 (alk. paper)
LC classification	RA771.7.R6 B3713 2018
Portion of title	Imagining rurality in Romania, 1860-1910
Subjects	Rural health--Romania--History--19th century. Rural health--Romania--History--20th century. Medicine, Rural--Romania--History--19th

	century.
	Medicine, Rural--Romania--History--20th century.
	Social medicine--Romania--History--19th century.
	Social medicine--Romania--History--20th century.
Notes	Includes bibliographical references and index.
Additional formats	Online version: Bărbulescu, Constantin, 1969- author. Physicians, peasants and modern medicine Budapest: New York: Central European University Press, [2018] 9789633862681 (DLC) 2018029609
	Online version: Bărbulescu, Constantin, 1969- author. Physicians, peasants and modern medicine Budapest: New York: Central European University Press, [2018] 9789633862681 (DLC) 2018029611
Series	CEU Press studies in the history of medicine; volume XII

Romania confronts its communist past: democracy, memory, and moral justice

LCCN	2018285831
Type of material	Book
Personal name	Tismaneanu, Vladimir, author.
Main title	Romania confronts its communist past: democracy, memory, and moral justice / Vladimir Tismaneanu (University of Maryland, College Park), Marius Stan (University of Bucharest, ICUB).
Published/Produced	Cambridge, United Kingdom: Cambridge University Press, 2018.
	©2018

Description viii, 205 pages; 24 cm

ISBN 1107025923 hardcover
9781107025929 hardcover
electronic bk.
electronic bk.

Related names Stan, Marius, author.

Summary Reckoning with mass crimes perpetrated by an ideologically driven regime entails engaging in a thorough exploration of its utopian foundations. In the case of Romania, such an analysis requires an interpretation of the role of personality in the construction of a uniquely grotesque and unrepentant forms of neo-Stalinist despotism. Of all the revolutions of 1989, the only violent one took place in Romania. Confronting its Community past therefore involves addressing the abuses committed by the Communist regime up until its very last day, its failure to engage in Round Table-type agreements with democratic representatives, and the repression during the first post-Communist years--a direct legacy of the old regime. This book shows how moral justice can contribute to a restoration of truth and a climate of trust in politics, in the absence of which any democratic polity remains exposed to authoritarian attacks--back cover.

Contents Introduction -- 1. Judging the Past in Post-Traumatic Societies: Romania in Comparative Perspective -- 2. Romania before 2006 -- 3. Coming to Terms with the Past in Romania: The Presidential Commission -- 4. Reactions to the Condemnation and Political Rearrangements after 2007 -- 5. The Report's Aftermath: Interpretations, Polemics, and Policies -- 6.

	Romania and the European Framework of Dealing with the Communist Past.
Subjects	1900-1999 Communism--Romania--History--20th century. Despotism--Romania--History--20th century. Communism. Despotism. Politics and government. Social conditions. Romania--Politics and government--1944-1989. Romania--Social conditions--1945-1989. Romania.
Form/Genre	History.
Notes	Includes bibliographical references and index.
Additional formats	Also available in electronic format. Electronic version: Tismaneanu, Vladimir. Romania Confronts its Communist Past. New York: Cambridge University Press, 2018 9781108574679 (OCoLC)1030820571

Social trends.

LCCN	2018213576
Type of material	Periodical or Newspaper
Uniform title	Social trends (Bucharest, Romania: 2018)
Main title	Social trends.
Published/Produced	Bucharest: National Institute of Statistics, 2018-
Publication history	Began with: 2018.
Description	volumes: color illustrations; 29 cm
LC classification	HQ1641 .T46
Continues	Tendințe sociale (Bucharest, Romania: 2017) (DLC) 2018213506 (OCoLC)1030584465
Related names	Institutul Național de Statistică (Romania), issuing body.
Subjects	Romania--Statistics--Periodicals.

Notes	Vols. for 2018- accompanied by CD-ROMs.

Staging citizenship: Roma, performance, and belonging in EU Romania

LCCN	2017276312
Type of material	Book
Personal name	Szeman, Ioana, author.
Main title	Staging citizenship: Roma, performance, and belonging in EU Romania / Ioana Szeman.
Published/Produced	New York: Berghahn Books, 2018. ©2018
Description	viii, 195 pages; 24 cm.
ISBN	9781785337307 hardcover 1785337300 hardcover
Portion of title	Roma, performance, and belonging in EU Romania
Summary	Based on over a decade of fieldwork conducted with urban Roma, Staging Citizenship offers a powerful new perspective on one of the European Union's most marginal and disenfranchised communities. Focusing on "performance" broadly conceived, it follows members of a squatter's settlement in Transylvania as they navigate precarious circumstances in a postsocialist state. Through accounts of music and dance performances, media representations, activism, and interactions with government agencies, author Ioana Szeman grounds broad themes of political economy, citizenship, resistance, and neoliberalism in her subjects' remarkably varied lives and experiences.
Subjects	Romanies--Romania--Social conditions. Culture conflict--Political aspects--Romania. Performing arts--Political aspects--Romania.

Romanies in mass media.
Culture conflict--Political aspects.
Ethnic relations.
Performing arts--Political aspects.
Romanies in mass media.
Romanies--Social conditions.
Romania--Ethnic relations.
Romania.

Notes Includes bibliographical references and index.

Series Dance and performance studies; volume 11
Dance and performance studies; v. 11.

The boy who cried vampire: a graphic novel

LCCN 2017020245

Type of material Book

Personal name Harper, Benjamin, author.

Main title The boy who cried vampire: a graphic novel / by Benjamin Harper; illustrated by Alex Lopez.

Published/Produced North Mankato, Minnesota: Stone Arch Books, a Capstone imprint, [2018]

ISBN 9781496554215 (library binding)
9781496554253 (pbk.)

LC classification PZ7.7.H366 Bo 2018

Related names Lopez, Alex, 1971- illustrator.

Summary In this graphic version of the classic fable, Ion is a boy in a little town in Transylvania who loves to play tricks on the other villagers, so when a real vampire appears at his window nobody responds to his cries for help, and it looks like the final trick is on Ion--maybe.

Subjects Fables--Adaptations--Comic books, strips, etc.
Fables--Adaptations--Juvenile fiction.
Vampires--Comic books, strips, etc.
Vampires--Juvenile fiction.

Practical jokes--Comic books, strips, etc.
Practical jokes--Juvenile fiction.
Graphic novels.
Graphic novels.
Fables.
Vampires--Fiction.
Practical jokes--Fiction.
Transylvania (Romania)--Comic books, strips, etc.
Transylvania (Romania)--Juvenile fiction.

Towards a jurisprudence of state communism: law and the failure of revolution

LCCN 2017041696
Type of material Book
Personal name Cercel, Cosmin Sebastian, 1982- author.
Main title Towards a jurisprudence of state communism: law and the failure of revolution / Cosmin Cercel.
Published/Produced Abingdon, Oxon; New York: Routledge, 2018.
ISBN 9781138684164 (hbk)
LC classification KKR464 .C47 2018
Contents Introduction -- Law before communism: modernity and the authoritarian drive -- A criticism of the heaven: class struggle and the law in theory and practice -- Revolution under siege: law, violence and marxist legal theory -- Revolution betrayed: the great retreat and the enduring legal canon -- The discourse of the master: war, law and the communist takeover -- Law as state-truth: the law-preserving violence and the limits of communism -- Exit communism: legal amnesia and the return of the repressed -- Conclusion.
Subjects Law--Romania--History--20th century.

Law and socialism--History--20th century.
Romania--Politics and government--1944-1989.
Notes Includes bibliographical references and index.

RELATED NOVA PUBLICATIONS

SELECTED ISSUES IN MACROECONOMIC AND REGIONAL MODELING: ROMANIA AS AN EMERGING COUNTRY IN THE EU

Editors: Emilian Dobrescu, Bianca Pauna, and Corina Saman
Center for Macroeconomic Modeling, National Institute of Economic Research "Costin C. Kiritescu," and Institute for Economic Forecasting, Romanian Academy, Bucharest, Romania

ISBN: 978-1-63484-936-4
Binding: Hardcover
Publication Date: 2016

This volume brings together eighteen studies on macroeconomic and regional modeling, dedicated to founding of the Macroeconomic Modelling Seminar of the Romanian Academy. All authors participated — at one time or another — in its business activity.

The first section is a collection of studies devoted to research on macroeconomics considered as a branch of economics that characterize the behavior of an economy as a whole. These studies focus on issues raised by modeling and forecasting aggregated indicators, such as industrial production, GDP growth rate, and price indexes (exchange rate, inflation) to understand how the economy functions. Exchange rate is one of the most important macroeconomic variables, especially in recent decades when the openness of the economies has grown due to the fact that development is based on competitiveness and international trade, and thus exposed them to exchange rate risk. Understanding underlying trends of inflation, focusing on expectations and the interaction among inflation, output growth and respective uncertainties are important problems in emerging countries, where the inflation is considered to be one of the main phenomena of instability of the economic environment, and the uncertainty about future inflation can lead to uncertainty about other economic variables.

These contributions from the researchers affiliated with the Macroeconomic Modeling Seminar gathered in this section propose some perspectives on these issues, emphasizing how econometric techniques can be used to model macroeconomic variables and how to capture uncertainty, structural breaks determined by the integration of Romania into EU, and/or by the latest major economic crises.

Several issues are hence considered, each emphasizing some aspects of the theme proposed: (i) forecasting exchange rate based on monetary fundamentals; (ii) capture uncertainties; (iii) understanding underlying trends of inflation, focusing on expectations; and (iv) assessing forecast accuracy for underlying models.

Performing analysis only at an aggregate level tends to obscure valuable information regarding regional disparities in terms of resources, economic development, socio-economic conditions. Therefore, there is a need to broaden the picture from national to regional in order to identify regional vulnerabilities, which is acknowledged by the articles from the second section of the volume.

The methodological section, the third and final volume, assembles some contributions that address specific issues about: (i) the measurement of jumps in high frequency data; (ii) the application of multiple attribute decision making models; (iii) the identification of the collinearity in regression models; (iv) the usefulness of Onicescu information energy together with the Shannon entropy to measure nominal variables; and (v) methodological advancements in the estimation of potential output.

WHAT/WHO ARE WE AFTER THE TRANSITION? FOCUS ON ROMANIA

Editors: Marin Dinu, Dorel Ailenei, Anca Dachin, Cătălin Huidumac-Petrescu, Mariana Iovițu, Marius-Corneliu Marinaș, Christina Marta Suciu, and Alexandru Bodislav
Bucharest University of Economics Studies, Bucharest, RO

ISBN: 978-1-63483-947-1
Binding: Hardcover
Publication Date: 2015

What/Who are we After the Transition? is not only an expression fit for a book title, but also a tense issue whose rational solutions are slow in coming amid the vibrating emotion for the life-changing consistency differential. The prospects of long processes cover a life expectancy, but in Romania, where generations of sacrifice succeeded one after another, time does not have enough patience to run smoothly.

The assessment made in this book is an attempt at decoding what has been done by the last generation, i.e., the transitional generation from communism to capitalism. The authors reunited under the Research and

Economic Analysis Centre part of the Department of Economics and Economic Policies from the Faculty of Theoretical and Applied Economics, which is part of the Bucharest University of Economics. In their analyses, the authors refer to the mental milestones of Romanian society that was built on frail social slopes. The different parts of Romanian society do not always agree with each other, between what we are and what we stand for as a people or as nation, between what we can and what we do, between what we want and what we have.

The topics referred to herein come with a bit of historical background, but they are approached starting with the need to explain why things happened this way and why it is not as we expected, from the standpoint of higher individual and societal amenities. The authors were driven by the moral burden to identify a progress-generating formula even under tough external constraints, stemming from any arrangement, conditionality or commitment undertaken by an open-economy country with Western geostrategic options.

BUILDING BLOCKS IN MODELING A MARKET ECONOMY: THE DOBRESCU MACROMODEL OF ROMANIA

Editors: Bianca Pauna and Corina Saman
Centre for Macroeconomic Modelling, National Institute for Economic Research (NIER), Romanian Academy

ISBN: 978-1-62808-551-8
Binding: Hardcover
Publication Date: 2013

In most countries there is a growing demand for forecasting tools, and Romania is no exception. The main forecasting tool used by the Romanian decision makers in order to construct prognosis for the economy or in order to analyze the effect of different policies is the 2005 Dobrescu Model. Although the Dobrescu macro-model has proved its usefulness, factors have pointed toward the need to update it.

This book presents an up-dated version of the Dobrescu Model of the Romanian economy, structured as independent blocks. The model consists of 6 blocks. In the main block, the main macroeconomic indicators are forecasted: the GDP and its components (with the exception of the budget expenses which are computed in the budget block), the labor market indicators (participation rate and unemployment rate), labor income, foreign trade and prices and the exchange rate.

The General Consolidated Budget block links the budget variables to other macroeconomic indicators from the main block, thus enabling an analysis of the implications that different policies might have on the budget. The budget revenues are connected directly to the legal rates, thus making possible the observation effect of tax changes. The approach permits the separation of the factors related to the macroeconomic environment and the factors related to fiscal policies.

The Monetary and Balance of Payments block is structured in two sub-blocks: the banking sector and external sector. The banking sector includes commercial banks and the central bank, and generates estimates for demand of money, dynamics of the non-governmental credit, active and passive interest rates. The external sector details variables related to the balance of payments like current account balance, foreign direct investment, net portfolio investment, total debt, medium and long-term debt, etc..

The Primary Energy Balance block aims to capture the effect of structural changes at the level of the economy's sector and household sector on the demand for energy. The block has behavioral equations for the households demand for energy, productive sectors' demand for energy and energy losses, which together made up the demand for energy. In this version of the model the production of energy together with energy imports are exogenous. In order to analyze the sustainability of the economic development an estimate of the green gases emissions is obtained as well.

The Sectoral Structure of the Economy block models the sectoral dynamics of the defined 10 branches of Romania's economy with the help of Input-Output tables. It uses inputs from the main block in the form of gross domestic product, gross fixed capital formation, exports, imports, etc., and the aggregate variable is decomposed into the 10 sectoral components.

The long term forecast block was introduced in order to quantify the long term effects of a different possible development path. The block is constructed using specific theories in order to provide long term forecasts of 10 to 15 years.

THE RE-EDUCATION EXPERIMENT IN ROMANIA: A SURVIVOR'S VIEWS OF THE PAST, PRESENT, AND FUTURE

Daniel Teodorescu[1] and Gheorghe Boldur-Latescu[2]
[1]Hunter College School of Education, New York, New York, US
[2]Academy of Economic Studies, Bucharest, Romania

ISBN: 978-1-62417-289-2
Binding: Hardcover
Publication Date: 2013

Very little is known--not only by the Western world but also by the Romanian youth--about the magnitude of the horrors the communist regime in Romania committed over its 40 years of dictatorship. This book is a collection of essays written between 1995 and 2011, chronicling the experiences and presenting the views of a former political prisoner about past and current events in Romanian history. A retired professor of operations research, Boldur-Latescu is one of the few survivors of the 'Pitesti Phenomenon', the experiment launched in the 1950's in communist prisons by the Romanian Securitate, which aimed at re-educating political prisoners through peer exerted torture. This book is a continuation of the analysis that started with "The Communist Genocide in Romania", published in 2005 by Nova Publishers) with a particular emphasis on the examination of the social, political, cultural, and economic evolution of Romania after the 1989 Revolution. Some of the essays go beyond the analysis of the Romanian context by tackling current challenges faced by Western democracies through a unique prism. The link between communism and terrorism, the lack of reference to Christian values in the EU Constitution, and the relevance of Tolstoy's work or the Testament left by Peter the Great to the current situation in world politics, are only a few examples of the author's unique interpretation of current world events.

Impact of Investments on an Emerging Economy: Models and Forecasts. The Case of Romania

Cornelia Scutaru
Institute of Economic Forecasting, Romanian Academy of Science
Bucharest, Romania

ISBN: 978-1-60876-182-1
Binding: Hardcover
Publication Date: 2013

This new book addresses the problem of correlations between investments, economic growth and employment using three different instruments: error correction models, neural networks and VAR models. Analysing the results, the authors conclude about the coherence of the three types of models wich have considered the reciprocal influences between investments and economic growth; investments and employment.

The factors with positive impacts (GDP growth, foreign direct investments, degree of imports coverage by exports, wage increase) and negative impacts (active interest rate, depreciation of the exchange rate, unemployment, increase in tax burden) upon investments were revealed and policy measures formulated.

THE COMMUNIST GENOCIDE IN ROMANIA

Boldur-Lăþescu, Gheorghe
Translated by Teodorescu

ISBN: 978-1-59454-251-0
Binding: Hardcover
Publication Date: 2005

At the end of December 1989, only a few days after the Romanian people and its admirable youth victoriously toppled Ceauşescu's dictatorship, I thought that my first duty as a scholar with expertise in economic cybernetics was to apply the methods of this modern discipline to research and develop solutions that would improve the economic situation in Romania, which had been virtually ruined by the aberrant communist system. In parallel with my own reflections on this critical mission, I built along with a team of enthusiastic colleagues a methodological model for economic restructuring. At that time, my hope was that our modest efforts, the first of this kind after the Revolution, would inspire other experts from the Academy of Economic Studies, where we were teaching, and from similar institutions throughout the nation, to join us in these efforts. I was expecting that through collaboration we would develop a model that could be utilized by our new leaders to guide Romania's macroeconomic policies. I have to confess that I was also hoping to capture the attention of the main political parties, which I was convinced they, too, were intensely preoccupied with finding solutions to overcome the disastrous economic situation in our country. Unfortunately, almost none of these ambitions materialized. With the exception of a brief coverage by a British TV station and several phone calls made by experts to ask for clarifications, there have not been any reactions—either positive or negative—regarding the possibility of approaching the issues of economic restructuring through the modern use of cybernetics. At the same time, every two or three days we were learning that another professor at my institution acceded to an important leadership position in either the academic, governmental, or parliamentary echelons. The time was ripe for the "climbers," those folks who profited from the instability inherent to a post-revolutionary situation, by aggressively seeking power, honors, or wealth, while ignoring the country's burning problems or approaching them through the prism of personal interests.

This desperate rat race for fast accession to power was occurring, unfortunately, at all levels of the society and it seemed as if from the state of grace the entire nation had experienced in the miraculous days of the Revolution, we rapidly entered a general state of confusion, deception, hatred, and violence.

Loneliness Among Romanian Immigrants Living in Portugal*

Félix Neto and Maria da Conceição Pinto
Department of Psychology, University of Porto, Portugal

This study approaches the determinants of loneliness among Romanian migrants living in Portugal. Two research questions guided the study:

* The full version of this chapter can be found in *Psychology of Loneliness: New Research*, edited by Lázár Rudolf, published by Nova Science Publishers, Inc, New York, 2017.

(1) What influences do acculturation problems have on loneliness? (2) What influences does adaptation to the society of settlement have on loneliness? The sample of this research consisted of 181 Romanian immigrants living in Portugal (49% females). The average duration of stay in Portugal was 9 years. Loneliness was measured by the ULS-6. In addition, other scales were used to assess Portuguese language proficiency, perceived discrimination, sociocultural adaptation, multicultural ideology, psychological problems and self-esteem. Results showed that both indicators of acculturation problems and of adaptation significantly predicted loneliness. Implications of the findings for future research are discussed.

THE ASSESSMENT OF POWER QUALITY IN ELECTRIC DISTRIBUTION SYSTEMS FROM ROMANIA*

Bogdan C. Neagu*[1]*, PhD and Gheorghe Grigoraş, PhD

"Gheorghe Asachi" Technical University of Iasi,

Faculty of Electrical Engineering, Iasi, Romania

The latest version of the European standard EN 50160 has been released in 2010 and it is applicable only under the steady-state of an electric distribution system. The voltage quality parameters (i.e., supply voltage magnitude, harmonic voltages and voltage unbalance) affect directly active and reactive power consumption and power losses in the

* The full version of this chapter can be found in *Advances in Energy Research. Volume 28*, edited by Morena J. Acosta, published by Nova Science Publishers, Inc., New York, 2017.

[1] Corresponding Author Email: bogdan.neagu@tuiasi.ro.

elements of electric distribution networks (lines and transformers). In the same time, the harmonics causes additional power loss, shorter insulation lifetime, higher temperature and insulation stress, reduced power factor, etc. From the viewpoint of operation, the supply voltage variations are very important.

These variations are the most common voltage quality problems in the steady-states. In terms of the supply voltage levels, these are different for every node (MV/LV electric substation) from the electric distribution network. The voltage variations are affected by customers' load structures and supply network characteristics such as transformer impedance, line impedance, voltage level etc. Also, because the LV distribution networks supply a significant number of nonlinear consumers which causes a distorted and unbalanced state, another negative effect is represented by the increase of power losses in network elements (lines and transformers). Even if the symmetrical sinusoidal state is initially considered for the power losses, in reality this often leads to power lines overloading, especially for the neutral.

Today, by using the information provided from the smart meters installed in the power substations the power quality indicators can be assessed with a high accuracy. In Romania, the implementation of smart metering in pilot rural and urban areas had the positive effects on power quality. The smart meters are able to capture the average values of voltage and currents.

The obtained information offers the base for an assessment of power quality indices in the whole LV network using Artificial Intelligence (AI) techniques. In this chapter, new and powerful tools based on AI techniques (clustering and fuzzy modeling) will be proposed for the assessment of slow voltage variations and harmonic content in the electric distribution systems.

Barriers towards Establishing Palliative Care in Eastern Europe and Prospects for Improvements in the Future: Romania as an Example*

Daniela Mosoiu[1], MD, PhD and Alexandru Eniu[2], MD, PhD

[1]Transilvania University, Brasov, Romania, Hospice Casa Sperantei, Brasov, Romania

[2]Cancer Institute Ion Chiricuta, Cluj-Napoca, Romania

Establishing an effective and accessible palliative care service in Eastern Europe encounters enormous barriers due to lack of financing, human resources and awareness. In a competing environment for scarce resources, in which priority is given to curative interventions, developing palliative services requires determination on the long term to change mentalities but also to actively engage into changing laws and regulations that do not favour the patients in need. Romania is an example where strong leadership from local champions that dedicated their time to advocate for the recognition of the true value of palliative services led to an important improvement in the post-communist era. Focusing on specialized and community clinical services' development, educational programmes and advancement of palliative care at national and international level make from Hospice Casa Sperantei an example that can be enlightening and inspiring for others in the area in taking the necessary steps towards implementing at national level services that offer much-needed relief for patients and their families. In a context of limited resources and continuous changing health policy, Hospice Casa Sperantei is looking for different solutions to develop services and overcome

* The full version of this chapter can be found in *Palliative Care: Perspectives, Practices and Impact on Quality of Life. A Global View. Volume 1*, edited by Michael Silbermann, published by Nova Science Publishers, Inc., New York, 2017.

barriers, such as: piloting models to test potential solutions for better care and build up towards a national strategy, developing quality improvement mechanisms and accreditation for palliative care providers, developing a national volunteering program.

ROMANIA'S STUDY CASE: NATIONAL BENCHMARKING COUNTIES REGARDING A SUSTAINABLE ECONOMIC GROWTH PROFILE USING THE WORLD BANK JOGG'S MODEL*

Cristina Lincaru[1,2,*], PhD, Vasilica Ciuca[2], PhD and Speranța Pirciog[2], PhD
[1]Department of Labour Market,
[2]National Scientific Research Institute for Labour and Social Protection, Bucharest, Romania

The New Economy of Geography explains how production is heterogeneously distributed in space, reflecting the tendency of agglomeration in highly populated locations (countries, regions, and localities) while also increasing the income in the same areas of success. This chapter is a piece in the line of research focused on the employment growth analysis in Romania in both quantitative and qualitative dimensions.

The novelty element of this work is represented by applying Step 1 from the World Bank Methodology known as JoGGs [1], [2] at the NUTS3 level in Romania. The JoGGs method was applied independently in all 42 counties for the period variation of 2010-2013. The JoGGs method was

---

* The full version of this chapter can be found in *Progress in Economics Research. Volume 38*, edited by Albert Tavidze, published by Nova Science Publishers, Inc., New York, 2017.

* Corresponding Author Email: cristina.lincaru@yahoo.de.

used to calculate the decomposition of the total VAB changes per capita at the county level with the Shapley method for three main components: productivity, employment and demography. These componentss reflect: (1) the growth linked with productivity as VAB changes per worker; (2) the growth linked with changes in employment rate (regardless of employment status in the labour market); and (3) the growth linked with the demographic factor that shifts in the share of population in the working age, ignoring the international mobility of labour. This model was applied for Romania at the national level by Lincaru (2015), who analysed different time intervals (1997-2008, 2008-2009, 2009-2014, 2007-2012 and 2012-2014). Shapley decomposition results and input indicators are used in achieving national benchmarking counties concerning sustainable economic growth profiles. An economic growth profile is compiled of each administrative unit based on the direct analysis of factors by applying the Shapley method at this level, using 24 indicators as input data and three indicators as output data. The JoGGs model was used as input data for each of the eight dimensions using the following three characteristics: the level in 2010, the level in 2013 and the growth rate in 2013 compared to 2010.

The national benchmarking of counties after a growth profile (which includes sustainable, smart and inclusive growth) is the result of an analysis based on a multi-criterial portfolio (using ranks and the normalization of the five classes of Jenks natural intervals by case).

In the post-crisis period (2010-2014) the convergence process (Eurostat data, [tgs00107]) is: visible for poorly performing regions (with mentioned indicator values above the national average – Southwest, Northeast and Muntenia Sud) and stagnant or not visible for five other areas.

The principal conclusions of this study are:

- Increasing regional disparities request a New Economic Growth Agenda at the regional level.
- The spatial perspective is vital to analyse the heterogeneities of sustainable, smart and inclusive economic growth.

ROMANIAN SUNFLOWER OIL: QUALITY INDICES, PHYSICAL – CHEMICAL PROPERTIES AND POTENTIAL APPLICATIONS*

Doina G. Andronoiu[1,†]***, Anisoara A. Neagu***[2]***,***
Gabriel D. Mocanu[1]***, Oana V. Nistor***[1]
and Elisabeta Botez[1]
[1]Department of Food Science,
Food Engineering and Applied Biotechnology,
Faculty of Food Science and Engineering,
"*Dunarea de Jos*" University of Galati, Galati, Romania
[2]Department of Chemistry and Chemical Engineering,
Faculty of Applied Sciences and Engineering,
"*Ovidius*" University of Constanta, Constanta, Romania

In 2011 sunflower oil represented the 4th consumed oil in the entire world, comprising almost 13% of the total oil types consumed. This type of vegetable oil is obtained from the seed of the plant *Helianthus annuus L.* Romania is one of the most significant oilseeds producer in Europe. In Romania the typical oil crops are represented by 66% sunflower seed, 30% rapeseed, 3% soybean and 1% for other type of crops. Sunflower oil represents the most important edible oil used in Romania.. In comparison with other edible oils, sunflower oil is a good natural source of tocopherols and phytosterols, this vegetable oil having the highest amount of α – tocopherol and β-sitosterol. This content of tocopherols and phytosterols, can vary with the genotype, plant variety and environmental factors. Sunflower oil is rich in polyunsaturated fatty acids (high content in linoleic

* The full version of this chapter can be found in *Sunflower Oil: Interactions, Applications and Research*, edited by Md Monwar Hossain, published by Nova Science Publishers, Inc., New York, 2017.

† Corresponding Author Email: gandronoiu@ugal.ro.

acid). It contains also high amounts of bioactive compounds, such as polyphenols (vanillic acid, caffeic acid, ferulic acid and sinapic acid), which play an important role in the prevention and treatment of some chronic diseases and improve immune function. Antioxidant and anti-inflammatory activities have been reported in a few studies about sunflower oil and were related to the presence of coenzyme Q9 (CoQ9) and CoQ10. Different indices and physical – chemical properties are used to evaluate the quality of edible oils. These indices include: acid value, saponification value, ester value and also the iodine and peroxide value. The physical and chemical properties used to establish the quality of sunflower oil are: density, dynamic viscosity and refractive index.

Sunflower oil is used on a large scale in area of food: for cooking, frying, margarine and spreads production, salad dressings, ice-cream, soups, bakery products, confectionery products and also as fat substitute for reformulated meat and dairy products. This chapter will present the quality indices, physical and chemical properties of sunflower oil and some potential applications in food products reformulation.

DOING BUSINESS IN EMERGING MARKETS: THE CASE OF ROMANIA[*]

Manuela Epure*[†]*, PhD and Aurelian A. Bondrea,PhD

Spiru Haret University, Academy of Romanian Scientists,
Bucharest, Romania

Doing business today seems to be a very challenging endeavor. Drivers such as globalization, technological changes, and the economic crisis, to

[*] The full version of this chapter can be found in *Business Models: Strategies, Impacts and Challenges*, edited by Adam Jabłoński, published by Nova Science Publishers, Inc., New York, 2016.

[†] Corresponding Author Email: mepure.mk@spiruharet.ro.

mention just a few are changing the game. The firms that are successful and fast growing in this rather hostile environment appear to be those that demonstrate a real capacity to compete "differently" and especially to innovate in their business models. Recent studies, such as IBM' s Global CEO Study, show that managers from a broad range of industries are interested in receiving guidance on how to innovate in their business models in order to improve their ability to create and capture value for their customers. It is widely recognized that for an organization to thrive, managers must have a good understanding of how business models work. The research community has, so far, only offered early insights on this issue and has not really focused on emerging markets.

In this international context, this chapter will provide new perspectives on doing business in emerging markets by exploring the most appropriate ways to develop an adaptive business model which would support firms on their path to success.

Emerging markets are now seen as a unique environment which requires a systematic approach to developing novel business models. Going global is one thing, but targeting emerging economies is quite a different story. Prestigious scholars have discussed strategy development, government interaction, the exploitation of local opportunities and risk management issues in emerging economies. Khanna and Palepu offer some guidelines for success in emerging markets, for example how to identify and respond to institutional voids of product, labour and capital markets and how investors and entrepreneurs can respond to niches in institutional infrastructure in the private sector. This is very interesting advice on how to present innovative products in order to attract emerging middle class consumers. When managers are asked what is distinctive about emerging markets, they typically point to rapid economic growth, potential competitors, and vexing problems including but not limited to corruption, financial crises, and weak intellectual property rights (Legace, 2010). But this is not the whole picture. The first part of this chapter will explore the features of emerging markets in terms of their business environment, with a special emphasis on Romania's case. Some important rating agencies place Romania as a "frontier" country, while others seem to agree on categorizing Romania as being amongst the emerging market countries. The findings of such an exploratory case study of Romania helped us to set-up a country profile of the business environment and became the starting point to identifying the pillars of a successful business model.

The chapter' s second part is dedicated to business model innovations in emerging markets by trying to define the meaning of innovation and how innovative business models have impacted both the customers and the market. Once innovation drivers are identified, the analysis goes deeper in order to identify the drawbacks and the kinds of regulations which might affect the stability of the business environment which could demand major shifts in business models.

The third part of the chapter will provide insights on Romania's business environment by looking at the key factors and tactics that have driven Renault's success as an automotive company. Dacia has represented a well-known car brand in Romaniasince the '60s and has become one of the most successful Renault brands worldwide. Their business model is analyzed in order to understand the ways in which it operates and how it creates value for its stakeholders. The generic two-stage competitive process framework will be employed and a business model representation is provided.

Finally, the case study focuses not only on the business model itself, but also on consumer perspectives. Intangible assets such as experience, brand equity and intellectual capital are important for any business. So how are these assets employed in order to build a successful business in an emerging market? Romanian specificities are described and their influence on the Renault business model is explored. Nevertheless, the chapter merely tackles the framework of doing business in an emerging market; further in-depth research is needed, especially the monitorisation of the business models evolution over time. Being successful as a company seems to equate with the design and implementation of an innovative business model which is easily adaptive to a specific market environment.

The Potential of Young People from Rural Communities in Romania*

Violeta Sima*† *and Ileana Georgiana Gheorghe
Petroleum-Gas University of Ploiesti,
Business Administration Department, Ploiesti, Romania

This chapter has started from the study of the main difficulties faced by the young people living in rural communities from Romania. The rural community inhabitants are part of the poorest in Romania, with poor access to services, reduced employment opportunities, but also with a low level of civic culture. The authors described the main worrying phenomena faced by the Romanian villages in the introduction. These phenomena are a low birth rate, an increase in total mortality and infant mortality, a decline in the number of marriages, a decline in the fertility rate, a decrease in the number of jobs, and a poor infrastructure. Taking into account the sustainable development definition, the authors highlighted the importance of studying the youth problems. The main body of the chapter attempted to highlight a profile of the young people from rural areas in Romania. In this regard, the authors have taken into account the main challenges faced by the young people in Romanian rural communities in the current context, namely social capital, human capital, national policies, malfunctioning of the public institutions, authorities, and legislation. The Romanian rural areas have a very high potential which remains still poorly exploited. Within the context of sustainable development, a more efficient use of the resources available in the rural area could contribute to the resurrection of Romanian traditions, and to the improving of the quality of the community

* The full version of this chapter can be found in *Rural Communities in the Global Economy: Beyond The Classical Rural Economy Paradigms*, edited by Istudor Nicolae, Ignacio de los Ríos and Andrei Jean Vasile, published by Nova Science Publishers, Inc., New York, 2016.

† Petroleum-Gas University, 39 Bucuresti St., 100680 Ploiesti, Romania; Email: violeta.sima@gmail.com.

living in these areas. Demographic policy formulation is essential for the whole social environment, generating influence on all aspects of life. More training opportunities, more numerous and more diversified jobs should be provided to rural young people, which will allow the preservation of the valuable potential of the young people in rural communities.

The Importance of Rural Tourism in Romanian Village Development*

***Adrian Ungureanu*†**

Petroleum-Gas University of Ploieşti, Prahova, Romania

Rural tourism is a complex activity, capable to determine mutations regarding the territorial profile development; from this angle, it is considered to be a method of attenuation for the interregional discrepancy, at a national and European scale.

Rural tourism is an important part of the Romanian tourism sector, under continuous development for the past twenty years. Identifying the development ways of this sector is very important and especially necessary due to the multitude of problems that the sector faces and impeding its development to its full potential. Tourism is an alternative and a necessity for the area social-economic recovery, its progress depending also on the national and local authorities assistance, but especially on the local community willing to change.

---

* The full version of this chapter can be found in *Rural Communities in the Global Economy: Beyond The Classical Rural Economy Paradigms*, edited by Istudor Nicolae, Ignacio de los Ríos and Andrei Jean Vasile, published by Nova Science Publishers, Inc., New York, 2016.

† Adrian Ungureanu: Petroleum-Gas University of Ploieşti, B-dul Bucuresti no. 39, 100680 Ploieşti, Prahova, Romania. Email: ungureanu_adrian2001@yahoo.com.

The Development of Rural Communities in Romania in the Context of European Policies*

Jianu Daniel Mureşan*[†] *and Mihail Vincenţiu Ivan
Petroleum-Gas University of Ploiesti,
Faculty of Economic Sciences, Romania

As a historic rule, the more industrialized the state, the quicker it went from taxing agriculture to subsidizing agriculture. For a very long time, rural policies in the European Union overlapped agricultural policies and the agricultural sector. Rural Europe was considered a sector, disregarding its spatial dimension.

Today, after several reforms, the rural development policy of the EU is adapted to the new EU policy framework reflected in the Europe 2020 Strategy focused on employment, economic growth, innovation, education, social inclusion and energy/climate issues.

Rural areas of Member States are very different, both geographically (landscapes, climate and natural resources) as well as economically and demographically. While some rural areas are among the most prosperous European areas, others are below the threshold of absolute poverty. In the Romanian agricultural sector, the structural imbalances (same as those in pre-accession times) are higher than in most EU states, making corrections more complicated. Romania still has two agricultures, unconnected and often divergent in terms of interests and which require different policies from the state.

So the European experience in rural development policy shows that it is necessary, now more than ever before, to respond to two complementary

---

* The full version of this chapter can be found in *Rural Communities in the Global Economy: Beyond The Classical Rural Economy Paradigms*, edited by Istudor Nicolae, Ignacio de los Ríos and Andrei Jean Vasile, published by Nova Science Publishers, Inc., New York, 2016.

† Petroleum-Gas University, 39 Bucuresti St., 100680 Ploiesti, Romania, Email: jianu_muresan@yahoo.com.

functions: sectorial and territorial. Starting from rural development to the regional and sectorial one, the homogenization of public policies is undesirable; however, their diversification is not, because the great value of the European space consists precisely in diversity.

INCREASING THE PERFORMANCE OF THE VEGETABLE CHAIN IN ROMANIA[*]

Nicolae Istudor, Raluca Andreea Ion[†] and Iuliana Dobre

The Bucharest University of Economic Studies,
Faculty of Agro-food and Environmental Economics, Romania

This chapter analyzes the level of performance of the vegetable chain in Romania and aims to investigate the role of the coordination mechanisms on chain performance: The subsidies system, agro-food markets (price), economic contracts, horizontal and vertical integration. The research questions are: 'What are the main weaknesses of the chain and how can they be solved?'; 'Which coordination mechanism brings the highest performance and how can it be implemented?' A documentary study has been carried out, using statistical data and results of previous research. It was observed that the weakest point of the vegetable chain is collecting products from numerous farmers who hold small areas and deliver reduced quantities of heterogeneous vegetables to the market. A solution seems to be the farmers' association in bigger entities able to deliver large quantities of products. Scenarios for their association are

[*] The full version of this chapter can be found in *Rural Communities in the Global Economy: Beyond The Classical Rural Economy Paradigms*, edited by Istudor Nicolae, Ignacio de los Ríos and Andrei Jean Vasile, published by Nova Science Publishers, Inc., New York, 2016.

[†] Corresponding Author Email: raluca.ion@eam.ase.ro.

developed in this chapter, in the form of a project that can be used as an example for farmers who want to set up a marketing cooperative and apply for structural funds in order to finance the investment.

A Real-Time Daily Coincident Indicator for Romanian Economy[*]

Marius Acatrinei*[†], *PhD
Institute for Economic Forecasting, Bucharest, Romania

We construct a real-time daily coincident indicator for Romanian economy by extracting information from an unbalanced panel of daily, monthly and quarterly data with the help of the Harvey accumulator. We use a mixture of financial and macroeconomic data. By using a dynamic factor model transposed in a state-space framework, we can extract the daily unobserved common component. The indicator is a measure of the Romanian business conditions. In the second part we apply a Bayesian Markov-Switching with three states to the indicator for inferring the turning points in the business conditions and measure the duration of the recessions. Since the results showed that the indicator may provide significant real time information about the state of the economy and about the disequilibria latently accumulating in the economy well before the official release of the GDP, the indicator may be used as an early warning indicator for economic distress for Romanian economy.

---

[*] The full version of this chapter can be found in *Non-Linear Modeling of the Impact of the Crisis on the Interactions among Financial Markets and Macroeconomic Variables in CEE Countries*, edited by Lucian Liviu Albu and Petre Caraiani, published by Nova Science Publishers, Inc., New York, 2016.

[†] Corresponding Author Email: marius.acatrinei@gmail.com.

Euro Adoption in Romania: Moving Faster or Moving Slower?*

Gabriela Drăgan†, PhD

Faculty of International Business and Economics,
Bucharest Economic University, Bucharest, Romania
General Director of the European Institute
of Romania, Bucharest, Romania

The "Greek crisis," which led to the creation of a new EU reformed economic governance framework, has also exposed the significance of structural problems of both the eurozone and the EU as a whole. Both the long-term sustainability of the euro area and the progress of the European integration process will strongly depend on the respect of new fiscal rules, stronger coordination of economic policies combined with structural reforms and, particularly, the EU capacity to reduce its internal economic divergences. Therefore, the temporary fulfillment of numerical convergence criteria could not be, by itself, a guarantee of entering the euro area. In the long term, it will be problematic to strictly ensure the nominal convergence for joining the eurozone without increasing the real convergence among all EU member countries (either from the euro or non-euro areas).

* The full version of this chapter can be found in *The Eurozone Enlargement: Prospect of New EU Member States for Euro Adoption*, edited by Yoji Koyama, published by Nova Science Publishers, Inc., New York, 2015.

† Corresponding Author: Gabriela Drăgan, PhD, Professor, Faculty of International Business and Economics, Bucharest Economic University and General Director of the European Institute of Romania, e-mail: gabriela.dragan@ier.ro.

ROMANIANS IN ITALY: THE LARGEST DIASPORA COMMUNITY*

***Antonio Ricci*†**
IDOS Study and Research Center

Romanian immigrants in Italy number more than 1 million, representing the largest diaspora community of that country. Romanians comprise almost 75% of all the EU immigrants in Italy and approximately 20% of the entire foreign presence in our country.

Italy and Romania share a long history of mutual migratory flow. At the end of the 19th century, a strong emigration from Italy to Romania - especially from areas of Italy which were controlled by the Austro-Hungarian Empire - contributed to the development of the country. Italians found jobs in the construction and railroad industries and their descendants were joined at the end of the 20th century by several thousands of new Italian emigrants, mainly entrepreneurs or workers who followed Italian enterprises, aiming to create "made in Italy" products at lower production costs.

In Italy the available statistics with regard to immigrants from EU Member States are fewer than those available for other immigrants. Since 2007, in fact, EU immigrants are no longer required to obtain a residence permit at the Ministry of Interior. Most of the statistics detailing third country immigrants are not available regarding EU citizen migration.

* The full version of this chapter can be found in *The Other Side of Italy: Immigration in a Changing Country*, edited by Francesco Pittau, published by Nova Science Publishers, Inc., New York, 2015.

† antonio.ricci@dossierimmigrazione.it

ORAL HEALTH AND THE QUALITY OF LIFE FOR ROMANIAN ORTHODONTIC PATIENTS*

Irina Zetu, Sorana Rosu†, Liviu Zetu and Mihnea Iacob
"Grigore T. Popa" University of Medicine and Pharmacy, Iasi, Romania

Objectives: *Psychosocial Impact of Dental Aesthetic Questionnaire* (PIDAQ) represents the only available tool for assessing the quality of life for the orthodontic patients. The research studied the relationships between the different aspects of orthodontic care planning, and validated the Romanian version of the PIDAQ questionnaire.

Material and methods: A transversal study was carried out on a sample of 1126 subjects, age ranging between 6 and 28 years old. The self-evaluation of the orthodontic esthetic perception was assessed with the PIDAQ index, and the orthodontic treatment need was measured with the IOTN index.

Results: Esthetic perception - 70% of the subjects are unsatisfied with the appearance of their dentition.

Orthodontic treatment need perception - All the subjects consider that they need orthodontic treatment.

Esthetic perception and orthodontic treatment need relationship - 40.16% of the subjects, which were unsatisfied with their dentition appearance, considered that they do not require an orthodontic treatment.

Esthetic perception and the esthetic component of IOTN correlation - Among the subjects, assessed as in need severe treatment, 80% were "Unsatisfied" or "Deeply unsatisfied" with their dentition.

Discussion: The scores of the different PIDAQ dimensions determined in our study, were comparable with those reported by other authors.

---

* The full version of this chapter can be found in *Oral Health: Anesthetic Management, Social Determinants, Role of Nutrition and Impact on Quality of Life*, edited by Julia Renee Barnes, published by Nova Science Publishers, Inc., New York, 2015.

† Corresponding Author Email: rosu_danut82@yahoo.com.

Conclusion: The PIDAQ questionnaire remains the only tool to assess the link between the dental-maxillary anomalies and the quality of life.

Our results demonstrate that the Romanian version of the PIDAQ questionnaire is a valid instrument in assessing the psychosocial impact of the dentition esthetics related to the malocclusion.

THE EMOTIONS INDUSTRY IN ONLINE ROMANIAN POLITICS: SELLING LEADERSHIP AND TRUST DURING THE 2012 PARLIAMENTARY CAMPAIGN[*]

Florenta Toader[†]

Doctoral Studies in Communication Sciences, National University of Political Studies and Public Administration, Bucharest, Romania

This chapter examines the emergence of personalized online communication in Romanian politics. In an era of significant changes such as the prevalence of mass communications, a decline in party membership and the decay of traditional electoral allegiances, politicians use emotional practices as a strategy aimed at bonding with citizens. Thus, it is worthwhile examining the nature of strategies implemented by political candidates to sell leadership and gain support by means of their social network sites. To investigate this topic, content analysis and dispositive analysis were applied to four Romanian politicians' Facebook pages during the 2012 parliamentary campaign. Findings indicate that emotions are personalized and mobilized through discursive strategies (e.g., confession, value judgment) and references to events and experiences that are meaningful to voters (myths, religion, tragedies, national holidays, etc.).

[*] The full version of this chapter can be found in *The Walk of Shame*, edited by Mira Moshe, published by Nova Science Publishers, Inc., New York, 2013.

[†] Corresponding Author Email: florenta.toader@yahoo.com.

The results of this research study offer a comprehensive view of the political emotions industry by analyzing both qualitative and quantitative data.

THE WALK OF SHAME TO THE PRESIDENCY: THE ROMANIAN CASE*

Nicoleta Corbu[1] *and Mira Moshe*[2]
[1]National University of Political Studies and Public Administration, Romania
[2]Ariel University of Samaria, Israel

Voting is essentially a process based on people's emotional reactions to events and characters presented during election campaigns, as well as during the time period between campaigns. This chapter discusses the way shame can be turned into a political advantage during a presidential campaign. Shameful events disclosed during election campaigns about the candidates can have a severe impact on voting. However, with the aid of a smart public relations campaign, and significant media "help", shame can elicit a boomerang effect that will eventually only help the candidate on his way towards winning the election. This might be accomplished by means of staging victimization of the candidate, followed by constant denial of the facts during the days following the disclosure. This chapter presents a case study from the 2009 Romanian presidential campaign. The incumbent (and future) president walked the walk of shame during the presidential election and managed to turn it to his advantage, eventually leading him to re-election as president for a second term. A special focus is placed on the role of the media in turning the walk of shame into a political strategy to help the candidate win the campaign.

* The full version of this chapter can be found in *The Emotions Industry*, edited by Mira Moshe, published by Nova Science Publishers, Inc., New York, 2014.

INDEX

G

H

I

J

L

M

N

O

P

Q

R

S

T

U

V

W

The European Union and its Debt Crises: The Deception of the Greeks

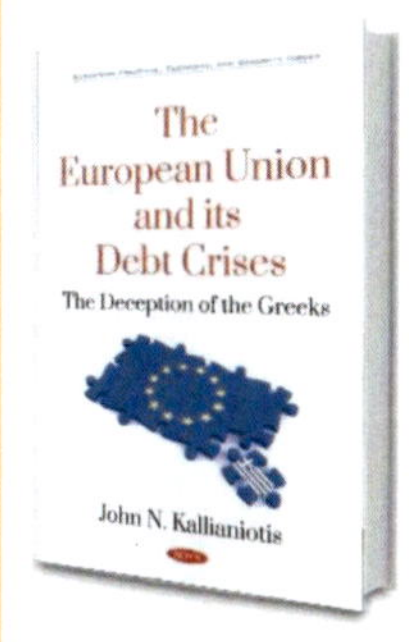

Editors: John N. Kallianiotis, University of Scranton, Scranton, PA

Series: European Political, Economic, and Security Issues

Book Description: *The European Union and its Debt Crises: The Deception of the Greeks* provides readers with in-depth historical, structural, political, and practical knowledge of the European Union, the Eurozone, and how to confront the latest financial, economic, and social problems.

Hardcover ISBN: 978-1-53614-067-5
Retail Price: $230

Slovakia: Culture, History and People

Editor: Tasha Wood

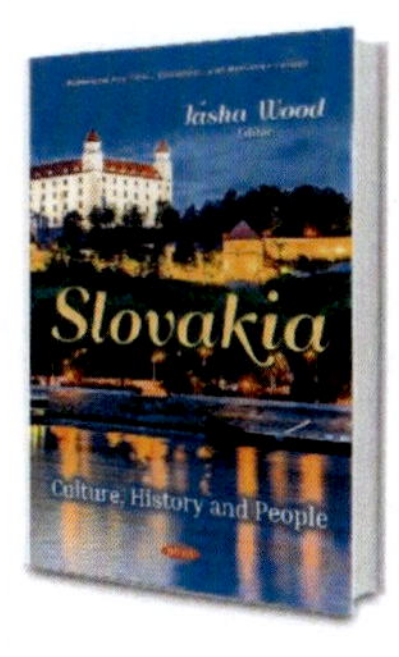

Series: European Political, Economic, and Security Issues

Book Description: In this compilation, the authors evaluate the political situation in Slovakia, a young democracy with a population of over five million and with history of a quarter of a century of independence lying in the heart of Europe, by analyzing the results of the recent general (parliamentary) election held in 2016 and a series of referenda that have taken place in Slovakia over the past two decades.

Softcover ISBN: 978-1-53614-133-7
Retail Price: $95

English Industries of the Middle Ages

Author: L. F. Salzmann

Series: European Political, Economic, and Security Issues

Book Description: This book, originally published in 1913, makes no pretense to be a complete history of the early industrial life of England, but at the same time it does claim to be an introduction to the study of that subject and provides more than a bare outline of industrial conditions in pre-Elizabethan days.

Softcover ISBN: 978-1-53613-604-3
Retail Price: $95

Lithuania: Political, Economic and Social Issues

Editor: Bronius Kazlauskas

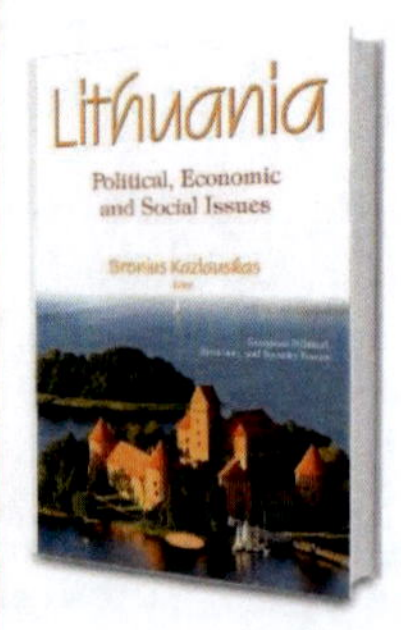

Series: European Political, Economic, and Security Issues

Book Description: Lithuanian economic, political and social development should be assessed from a historical perspective because Lithuania regained its independence in 1990 when the Soviet Union collapsed. *Lithuania: Political, Economic and Social Issues* opens with an analysis of the three stages of political, economic and social development in the period of Lithuanian independence.

Softcover ISBN: 978-1-53614-278-5
Retail Price: $95

A History of Police in England

Author: Captain W. L. Melville Lee

Series: European Political, Economic, and Security Issues

Book Description: This book, originally published in 1901, provides a thorough account of the English police system at the beginning of the twentieth century and offers many points of view that are relevant today.

Hardcover ISBN: 978-1-53614-226-6
Retail Price: $230

Russia: Background, Issues and Recent Developments

Author: Ulyana Asya Romanov

Series: European Political, Economic, and Security Issues,
Asian Political, Economic and Social Issues

Book Description: The first chapter examines Russia's 2018 presidential election, in which Russian President Vladimir Putin was widely expected to secure reelection (and since then, has won).

Hardcover ISBN: 978-1-53614-266-2
Retail Price: $160

An Introduction to the Industrial and Social History of England

Author: Edward P. Cheyney

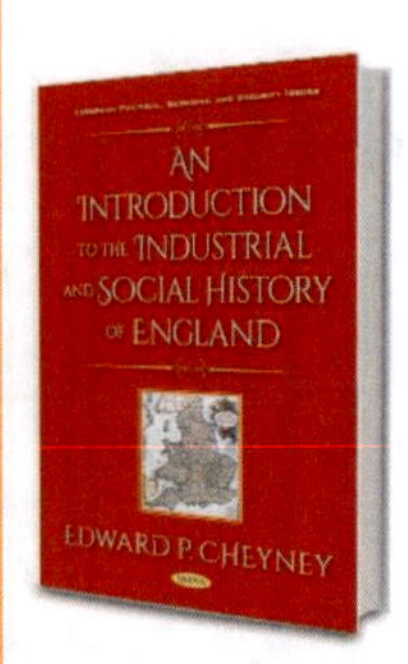

Series: European Political, Economic, and Security Issues

Book Description: This book, originally published in 1901, provides an introduction to the industrial and social history of England from prehistoric times to the early nineteenth century. Topics discussed include: the organization or rural life and town life; medieval trade and commerce; the Black Death and the Peasants' Rebellion; the end of the medieval system; the expansion of England; the Industrial Revolution; the extension of government control; and the extension of voluntary associations, trade unions, and trusts.

Hardcover ISBN: 978-1-53613-684-5
Retail Price: $230

Monetary Unions: Background, Advantages and Disadvantages

Author: Sławomir Ireneusz Bukowski, Kazimierz Pulaski University of Technology and Humanities in Radom, Poland

Series: European Political, Economic, and Security Issues

Book Description: This book embraces the problems of theoretical and historical fundamentals of monetary union with special concentration on the euro area, and discusses concerns of nominal and real convergence within the Economic and Monetary Union in the Europe, as well as problems of fiscal and monetary policy in the euro area.

Hardcover ISBN: 978-1-53614-250-1
Retail Price: $230